gay

a guide

...

peter jones, will mcloughlin, ian martin, andrew wyllie
photographs by heike löwenstein

gay london

a guide

••• ellipsis

•••

All rights reserved. No part of this publication may be reproduced in any form without written permission from the publisher

BRITISH LIBRARY CATALOGUING IN PUBLICATION
A CIP record for this book is available from the British Library

PUBLISHED BY •••ellipsis
2 Rufus Street London N1 6PE
www http://www.ellipsis.com
SERIES EDITOR Tom Neville
SERIES DESIGN Jonathan Moberly
EDITOR Vicky Wilson

COPYRIGHT © 1999 Ellipsis London Limited
ISBN 1 899858 73 3

FILM PROCESSING Metro

PRINTING AND BINDING Hong Kong

•••ellipsis is a trademark of Ellipsis London Limited

For a copy of the Ellipsis catalogue or information on special quantity orders of Ellipsis books please contact
Lindsay Evans
0171–739 3157 or lindsay@ellipsis.co.uk

1999

contents

0 introduction
1 areas
2 bars and cafés
3 clubs
4 hotels and restaurants
5 en plein air
6 cruising
7 baths/gyms/saunas
8 shopping
9 markets
10 museums and galleries
11 theatres and concerts
12 events
13 index

Introduction

> When a man is tired of London he is tired of life; for there is in London all that life can afford.
> Samuel Johnson

There are many unselective guides available to London's gay bars, clubs, saunas and cruising grounds. But London offers more than this, and *Gay London* provides a carefully mapped journey through the capital's gay scene and the city that surrounds it. Instead of a comprehensive listing of gay London life, it aims to draw attention to the best the scene has to offer and to recommend to the gay visitor or resident a number of eclectic cultural gems and special places within the city – viewed, of course, through a gay lens. Gay venues are reviewed in some depth and from an individual and subjective (but impartial in that no advertising revenue has greased our palms) perspective. But as Andrew Wyllie points out in his entry on First Out café, we've come to associate gay life perhaps too much with the scene, when in fact being queer doesn't happen only on licensed premises or at night. So *Gay London* includes museums, concerts, theatres, gardens, markets and even a boat trip that have been observed to attract a higher-than-average gay clientele, have a particular appeal for a queer audience, or give an insight into the little-known history of homosexuals within the capital.

Decisions about what to include and what to leave out were not always easy. But on the whole we rejected characterless pubs and run-of-the-mill clubs for venues that display an independence of spirit and style – whether or not that conformed with our own tastes. Outside the scene, we opted for places that might reveal to residents and visitors alike a face of London often hidden, whether the 'scary industrial back-side' of Andrew Wyllie's Thames boat trip or the celebration of the gay

Introduction

contribution to British politics, arts and science provided by Will McLoughlin's queer reading of the National Portrait Gallery. Or we've chosen places we believe (from experience) gay men appreciate – the Arabian Nights fantasy of Leighton House; the anti-municipal charm of the Chelsea Physic Garden; the over-the-top extravagance of Glyndebourne; the gender-fuck of the Lyric, Hammersmith; the subtle stalking ground that is Columbia Road Flower Market. Many of these reveal facets of London that taken together give the city its individual character. And as Peter Jones says in his write-up of Balans West restaurant, there's nothing like infiltrating the straight world and turning it queer.

As Samuel Johnson recognised, London offers all a man might need – a dazzling range of aesthetic, offbeat, cultural and hedonistic activities perhaps unparalleled by any other capital. The city is renowned for its excellent theatre and concert programmes – though the adventurous fringe fare of the Drill Hall, the combination of scruffy do-goodery and musical professionalism offered by Conway Hall and the pastoral delights of the Kenwood and Holland Park music festivals reach beyond the usual tourist itinerary. (And if you're interested in more traditional drama, the doyennes of drag still clump the boards on a regular basis at Central Station and the Royal Vauxhall Tavern.) A stroll around the City can be the occasion for a visit to an astonishing number of Wren churches, many of which you'll have entirely to yourself. And the history of the capital supplied by the Museum of London or the 'queen's tent' that is the Soane Museum are treasures discovered by only a discerning few (that is, until all our readers turn up).

We assume you'll want to take care of needs other than the cultural or spiritual, so though only two restaurants (Balans West and The Peasant) have individual write-ups, many entries include information

Introduction

about where to eat and drink nearby. (And for those of you more interested in punishment than pleasure, gyms are included too.) More solitary pursuits with a frisson of excitement can be found at Hampstead Heath or Abney Park and Brompton cemeteries, where a chance encounter with a fallen angel can be gratifying in more ways than one. And the cultural richness of London crosses ethnic as well as high/low, gay/straight divides, as a trip to Camden Market or Brick Lane – sadly, the target of a vicious racist bomb attack in April 1999 – will reveal.

As far as the scene itself is concerned, gay London has expanded beyond recognition in the last decade. Though queer-only and men-only enclaves such as the leather-fetish club Backstreet or the Aquarius sauna in Streatham still exist (and may be just what a man needs from time to time), many venues and events are now mixed les/gay or mixed les/gay/straight. Gay entrepreneurs have opened restaurants, upmarket, uptown bars, shops and trend-conscious clubs. Gone are the days when gay venues were entered via discreet side doors and open only to those in the know – today a combination of upfront visibility and commercialism has led to the creation of a gay village centred on Old Compton Street in Soho as well as the increased 'pinking' of such areas as Earl's Court and Islington. But more traditional venues and values can still be found – whether at the Black Cap, the Coleherne or on Ian Martin's East End pub crawl – while success stories such as Central Station prove that commerce and community are not mutually exclusive concepts. The bomb planted in the Admiral Duncan pub in Old Compton Street early on a Friday evening at the start of the 1999 May bank holiday in an attempt to kill or maim as many gay people as possible – following similar, racially motivated, attacks in Brixton Market and Brick Lane – shows that England still has its share of bigots, though the action drew

Introduction

universal condemnation from the establishment, and even a visit to the site by Prince Charles.

As you will discover when you read this book, *Gay London* was written by four men with very different tastes and interests. We have made no attempt to suppress these differences – the gay community encompasses all of us, and we hope you too will find your passions and pleasures catered for by the overlaps and combinations of the discreet voices.

So go out and enjoy.

ACKNOWLEDGEMENTS
Thanks to Jesus María Valeiras, Judith Scott and Tony Coghan.

The Gay Press

As the gay scene slowly moves out of the ghetto with an increasingly wide range of neo-post-gay venues, one certain way to tell if you're in a bender bar is to look around for the gaypers.

London's gay newspapers are freesheets that cover their costs from personal and public advertising. You don't pick up these papers for the quality of their journalism: they have very tight deadlines and they're chronically underfunded, so much so indeed that sometimes it seems they can't even afford basic spell-check software. On the other hand, they're in touch, they're up-to-date, and they're everywhere.

Titles come and go: *Axiom News* (originally intended to serve the HIV+ community) may survive the transition to a mainstream magazine and become a successor to the largely lamented *Capital Gay*; *Metropolis* (formerly *Thud*) died quietly at the end of 1998.

The Pink Paper is the closest thing to a gay paper of record. Its quasi-national circulation survives largely by virtue of its politically correct share of public-sector recruitment advertising, so it tends to eschew the escort ads and club-oriented dizzy-queen journalistic style that characterise its rivals – and is considered rather boring as a result.

Boyz, as its name implies, aims for a much younger crowd. The streetwise laddy tone that made it so much fun under its previous editor has paled a little under new management, but its geographically arranged listings are still the best source of information about who's doing what where and when. (A note of warning though: these papers rarely have the money to keep their databases accurate, so don't plan any major expeditions without asking around or ringing ahead.)

The London-only *QX*, which grew out of New York's distinctly club-oriented *MX* magazine, is smaller, ruder and stranger than either of the above – possibly because, unlike the others, it goes to press on Monday

The Gay Press

night, when half the staff are still suffering from the effects of the previous weekend. No magazine that survives on advertising revenue will ever be able to afford to be totally frank in its reviews of clubs and bars, but QX is often franker than most: 'We were so trashed by the time we got there that we don't remember much about it' is a much nicer way to describe an empty bar than 'refreshingly spacious'.

These gaypers arrive in pubs, bars and clubs late on Wednesday or Thursday evening. Just like the rest of us, they spend the weekend sitting around waiting to be picked up and taken home. And, just like the rest of us, by Monday or Tuesday they're trashed. Sic transit gloria gaynor. IM

HIV/AIDS Resources

AIDS TREATMENT PROJECT
Telephone 0645–470047
Monday to Wednesday, 18.00–21.00
Also publishes *Positive Treatment News*, newsletter/information sheet

CARA TRUST
178 Lancaster Road, London W11
Support for people with HIV/AIDS

ICARE
23–26 St Alban's Place, London N1 0WX (0171–359 7829)
Confidential service for people living with or affected by HIV/AIDS

THE TERRENCE HIGGINS TRUST
Telephone 0171–831 0330
Advice and information for people with HIV/AIDS

CLINICS
ARCHWAY SEXUAL HEALTH CLINIC
Whittington Hospital, Highgate Hill, London N19
(0171–5800/2804)

CENTRAL MIDDLESEX HOSPITAL, PATRICK CLEMENTS CLINIC, GUM DEPARTMENT
Acton Lane, London NW10 (0181–453 2221)

CHARING CROSS HOSPITAL GUM DEPARTMENT
Fulham Palace Road, London W6 (0181–846 1577)

HIV/AIDS Resources

CROYDON HIV COUNSELLING AND TESTING SERVICE
Broad Green Centre, 1-13 Lodge Road, West Croydon
(0181-684 2085)

EALING HOSPITAL, PASTEUR SUITE, INFECTION & IMMUNITY DEPARTMENT
8th Floor, Uxbridge Road, Southall (0181-354 5454)

GREENWICH DISTRICT HOSPITAL GUM DEPARTMENT
Vanbrugh Hill, London SE10 (0181-312 6056/858 8141 x6271 helpline)

KING'S COLLEGE HOSPITAL, CALDECOT CENTRE, DEPARTMENT OF SEXUAL HEALTH
15-22 Caldecot Road, London SE5
(0171-346 3453 GU clinic/3448 HIV outpatients)

KOBLER CLINIC
Ground Floor/1st Floor, St Stephen's Centre, 369 Fulham Road, London SW10 (0181-846 6161)
HIV COMMUNITY LIAISON TEAM
Telephone 0181-746 8235/8237/8238
Information and advice on how to access community health services, social services and voluntary organisations

MORTIMER MARKET CENTRE, GUM DEPARTMENT
off Capper Street, London WC1
(0171-530 5000/5050 appointments/5111 advice)

HIV/AIDS Resources

QUEEN MARY'S UNIVERSITY HOSPITAL, ROEHAMPTON CLINIC, DEPARTMENT OF SEXUAL HEALTH
Roehampton Lane, London SW15 (0181-789 0799/6611 x2470)

THE ROYAL FREE HOSPITAL, MARLBOROUGH CLINIC, GUM DEPARTMENT
Pond Street, London NW3
(0171-830 2047 appointments/794 0500 x3082 AIDS consultant)
IAN CHARLESON DAY CENTRE
Telephone 0171-830 2062/2051 (appointments)
HIV/AIDS UNIT
Telephone 0171-794 9599 x5076

THE ROYAL LONDON HOSPITAL, AMBROSE KING CENTRE, GUM DEPARTMENT
Turner Street, London E1
(0171-377 7306 direct line/7307 recorded information)

ST BARTHOLOMEW'S HOSPITAL GUM DEPARTMENT
First Floor, Horder Wing, West Smithfield, London EC1
(0171-601 8090)
ANDREWES UNIT
Telephone 0171-601 7738

ST GEORGE'S HOSPITAL, COURTYARD CLINIC, GUM DEPARTMENT
Blackshaw Road, London SW17 (0181-725 3353/3354)

ST MARY'S HOSPITAL, JEFFERISS WING, CENTRE FOR SEXUAL HEALTH
Praed Street, London W2 (0171-886 6618/6619)

HIV/AIDS Resources

UNIVERSITY COLLEGE HOSPITALS GROUP
Middlesex Hospital, Mortimer Street, London W1
(0171-636 8333 x4116/x4936)

WHIPPS CROSS HOSPITAL DEPARTMENT OF SEXUAL HEALTH
Whipps Cross Road, Leytonstone, London E11 (0181-535 6535)

Resources

LONDON LESBIAN AND GAY SWITCHBOARD
24-hour information and advice service; easier to get through to in the evening
0171-837 7324

CARELINE
Confidential counselling service for people worried about sexuality, relationships and AIDS
Monday to Friday, 10.00–16.00 and 19.00–22.00
0181-514 1177

GLAD Gay and Lesbian Legal Advice
Free confidential legal advice, information and referrals
Monday to Thursday, 19.00–21.30
0171-837 5212

HALL CARPENTER ARCHIVES
National gay and lesbian archives founded in 1982 with cuttings dating back to 1937
BM Archives, London WC1N 3XX (0181-686 7217)

LONDON FRIEND
Lesbian and gay helpline for information and support
Daily, 19.30–22.00
0171-837 3337

Resources

OUTLOOK LESBIAN AND GAY TALKING DIRECTORY
Business service, hotels, venues, etc
Monday to Saturday, 9.00–21.00; Sunday, 10.00–16.00
0800–298 8000

PACE
Counselling and advocacy for lesbians and gay men
Monday to Friday, 10.00–13.00 and 14.00–17.00
0171–697 0014 (counselling)/0016 (workshops)/0017 (advocacy)

areas

**Earl's Court 1.2
Islington 1.6
Old Compton Street 1.12**

Earl's Court

This area is one of the few places apart from East Soho (see page 1.12) with sufficient gay venues to create a community feel. Situated on the edge of wealthy Kensington, Earl's Court had a reputation in the 1940s and 1950s as a stopover point for newly arrived immigrants – Earl's Court Road was known as the Polish Corridor – and it is still popular today with young Australian travellers, who fill up its many hostels and cheap hotels, often oblivious to the gay scene. That said, Earl's Court Road is far posher than it was five or ten years ago and the seedier gay bars that used to stand alongside the Underground have disappeared in favour of high-street chains and brewery pubs. The main gay drag along Old Brompton Road consists of four major venues: Balans West (see page 4.2), the Coleherne (see page 2.8), Clone Zone and Bromptons. Just beyond Bromptons is Brompton Cemetery (see page 6.4), a major cruising ground.

Anyone wishing to sample the pleasures of a world gone by might pass along Coleherne Road down the side of the Coleherne pub to marvel at the window of Adonis Art. Got up like a respectable commercial gallery, this place has silly paintings of nude boys riding swans, plastic-looking marble busts and too much gilding. This stuff was the staple of the gay press in the 1970s and 1980s before we learned to be proud of porn.

Across Old Brompton Road from the Adonis, Clone Zone sells the real thing: a broad selection of soft gay porn and the paraphernalia of gay fetish – a range of athletic supporters, harnesses, exotic lubes, pumps, dildos, a rainbow of coloured hankies (for those nights at the Coleherne) and racks of whips and leather and rubber gear. Downstairs are sunbeds – £8 for ten minutes or 12 months unlimited usage for £325. It's no good being furtive in this place; the best approach is a teasing breeziness, pick the things up and HANDLE them for goodness' sake.

Earl's Court

areas

Earl's Court

Exiting right from Clone Zone and crossing over Warwick Road will bring you to Bromptons, Earl's Court's swinging hot spot. The upstairs bar is a good place to start earlyish: there are comfy sofas and a bit of Motown that, come 23.00 when the lights dim, lurches ill-advisedly into the Weather Girls. The crowd is largely Coleherne overspill at first, though many are younger. (Straight in from Heathrow on the Piccadilly line, Earl's Court is the first fleshpot the air crews hit coming off the plane.) Downstairs is a long bar area and a smoky, overcrowded dance-floor, very nice if neon, dry ice and endless piano keys are your thing (come on, you only need a sniff of poppers to get you there).

Scoring in Bromptons is like falling off a log – I defy anyone not to get cruised. A whole bevy of slightly imploring men with dolefully reproachful, expectant eyes are just waiting to take you home. PJ

ADONIS ART
ADDRESS 1B Coleherne Road, London SW10 (0171-460 3888)
OPEN Monday to Friday, 10.30–18.30; Saturday, 10.30–17.00

CLONE ZONE
ADDRESS 266 Old Brompton Road, London SW5 (0171-373 0598)
OPEN Monday to Saturday, 11.00–19.00; Sunday, 12.00–16.00

BROMPTONS
ADDRESS 294 Old Brompton Road, London SW5 (0171-370 1344)
OPEN Monday to Saturday, 18.00–2.00; Sunday, 18.00–24.00
ACCESS free before 23.00; Monday to Thursday £2.50 after 23.00; Friday and Saturday £3.50 after 23.00

UNDERGROUND Earl's Court

Earl's Court

areas

Islington

Islington has long held a reputation as one of London's most gay-friendly boroughs; more recently it has become one of its trendiest, home to writers, actors and politicians and watering hole for New Labour's finest.

Sir Francis Bacon, essayist, poet and politician, renowned for his love of 'ganymedes', lived on Canonbury Place in Canonbury Tower, now a theatre used primarily by the local (and very professional) amateur dramatic group.

Playwright Joe Orton lived at 25 Noel Road. Orton and his lover, Kenneth Halliwell, were sent to prison in 1962 on a charge of 'wilfully damaging' 83 library books and removing 1653 plates and illustrations. They had used the illustrations to create surrealistic collages to decorate their bedsit walls; they were also wont to doctor book jackets then lie in wait to observe the public's reaction. Three such books appeared as evidence at the trial: a biography of John Betjeman graced with a picture of an old man wearing swimming trunks and covered in tattoos; a book on etiquette with a female nude on the cover; and *Collins Guide to Roses*, adorned with a gorilla peering out from behind some rose petals. The books can still be seen at the public library at 2 Fieldway Crescent, just off Holloway Road. On Saturdays tourists stare up at the window where Halliwell brought their relationship, and Orton's life, to an end with a downward stroke of a hammer. Benjamin Britten and Peter Pears were other notable Islington residents, as is Chris Smith, the gay Secretary of State for Culture, Media and Sport and Britain's first openly gay MP.

The main drag – Upper Street – has a plethora of cafés, bars and restaurants as well as theatres and exhibition spaces. At the Angel end, Rosebery Avenue is the site of the newly reconstructed Sadler's Wells theatre, which reopened in 1998 and hosts an international programme of contemporary dance and ballet. The Kings Head pub theatre at 115 Upper Street

Islington

areas

Islington

often features productions which bend received notions of gender and sexuality. The Almeida on Almeida Street has in recent years attracted the likes of Diana Rigg, Ralph Fiennes and Juliette Binoche to pace its boards. And Union Chapel in Compton Avenue at the Highbury end of Upper Street, originally a non-conformist place of worship, is now a performance space featuring concerts in a dramatic gothic setting.

At 44A Pentonville Road is the Crafts Council of Great Britain, a fine neo-classical building hosting regular exhibitions of contemporary design and craft with a bookshop and café. In Canonbury Square is the Estorick Collection of Modern Italian Art. On Wednesdays and Saturdays there is an antiques market in Camden Passage, off Islington Green, where you can still find a bargain among the costume jewellery, silver, brass, ceramics, Victoriana and memorabilia.

Though none of the pubs on Upper Street itself has as yet succumbed to the lure of the pink pound, the area has no shortage of gay venues. In addition to The Angel (see page 2.2) and Central Station (see page 2.6), it's worth checking out the Edward VI on Broomfield Street (popular, mainly men, with a café/restaurant upstairs and a garden); the Ram Club Bar, appropriately located on Old Queen Street off Essex Road (friendly, mixed crowd, with pool table and garden); the Artful Dodger at 139 Southgate Road (traditional, youngish, male/female clientele, busy at weekends and on party nights); and the Duke of Wellington at 119 Balls Pond Road (traditional lesbian and gay pub with pool table).

There are restaurants to suit all tastes and pockets. At the top end of the price range, try Granita at 127 Upper Street for modern minimalist French/Californian cuisine; Lola's (The Mall, 359 Upper Street) for French cuisine and stylish, upmarket eating companions; the Peasant (see page 4.12); and Kavanagh's at 26 Penton Street, a small, gay-friendly

Islington

areas

Islington

space that does a great Sunday lunch. In the middle range are Le Mercury (140A Upper Street), a pleasant, very busy European restaurant; Gallipoli (102 Upper Street), a Turkish eaterie that serves excellent lamb in a fun atmosphere; Le Montmartre (26 Liverpool Road), a small, pleasant French bistro; or the Dome (341 Upper Street) for simple French food and snacks. At the lower end there's Pizza Express (335 Upper Street), with excellent views over the street for people-watching; Cafe Olé (119 Upper Street), a small, friendly pasta restaurant with very good sauces; and Charminar Vegetarian at 21 Chapel Market, which does a wonderful and very cheap buffet. WM

ADDRESS Upper Street, London N1
UNDERGROUND Angel, Highbury & Islington

Islington

areas

Old Compton Street

In iconic terms, this is perhaps the most important place in this book. It is *the* street, it is 'our' street – our Christopher Street, our Castro. But it is faster, and, despite its lack of political clout, sufficiently cosmopolitan to make America's main gay streets look positively provincial.

Old Compton's peculiar luck is its position at the convergence of several of London's busiest areas: literally a block from Chinatown, the theatres and cinemas and Covent Garden, and five minutes from Oxford Street and Piccadilly. Flanked by the wealthy blocks of Mayfair to one side and Covent Garden to the other, this area was until the mid-1980s London's premier red-light district. Then, as the sex shops were closed down, the restaurants moved in and the area developed a cache of swish eateries. Money flowed in, and Old Compton Street's pivotal position meant the first gay businesses fed into the mainstream, queering up the streets around them. Gradually the area changed from a place where you would meet gay people to a place where everyone seemed to be gay. The street has come to represent a tremendous freedom for gay men (and it is still largely a male affair) – the one public place in London where you can kiss your lover without fear of reprisal. Even the bomb attack in spring 1999 only served to make the community stronger. It's a street that has seen it all, a street where everyone has been, a short, buzzy catwalk where everyone catches your eye. A place that is, for all its faults, alive.

And yet, of course, like so much of gay London it does not represent all of us. The shamelessly aspirational gay-lifestyle vibe and the lack of any real women's venue means Old Compton is as exclusive for some as it is embracing for others. Nothing is so dismal as the annual 'carnival' weekends organised by the local bars and drag queens, nothing so unrepresentative, nothing less like a festival. And many would say that trawling the same bars can be just as joyless.

Old Compton Street

areas

Old Compton Street

Yet even the most die-hard queer anarchist must experience a slight frisson when passing down this street. For this is a public space where there are more of us than there are of them – an empowering idea to take back to all those other streets where we are not the majority. However much you may resist it, a little bit of Old Compton goes with you.

For the mainstream bars and restaurants the street is best seen on a Friday night somewhere between 22.00 and 23.00, or for a more romantic view see it on Saturday night/Sunday morning around 2.00, when all the lights of London seem to be winking at you.

The Old Compton Café, one of the earliest 1980s venues on the street, is the place to go when everywhere else has closed for the night. It also makes a great place to rendezvous between clubs. This cramped, bright space has a buzz about it 24 hours, very fast service and sandwiches good enough to pull in the local office workers. A little further down is Clone Zone (see also page 1.2): upstairs sells cards, books and some clingy T-shirts and underwear, downstairs fetishist bric-a-brac, sex toys, rubber, leather and (soft) porn. The shop is busy and relatively friendly, but best is the window that faces on to the street – often downright vulgar, it occasionally manages to make you laugh. Next door is Balans (see also page 4.2). The epitome of the early-1990s gay lifestyle, this brightly decorated bar/restaurant is always packed and has a glass frontage that opens in warmer weather and allows for street cruising. Beware though, it is known to host cabaret.

Across the road is Comptons, for a long time the only modern gay pub on the street. A couple of disastrous makeovers have turned a regular boozer into a cross between an American saloon (note the imposing wooden staircase) and mid-1970s suburbia (those carpets). Set out over two floors, each with a sizeable bar, the place seems to be sufficiently large

Old Compton Street

areas

Old Compton Street

'and tasteless to encourage a kind of wantonness in the clientele. Once through Comptons' portals you will be consumed by a passion for swilling down huge quantities of beer and leering at passers-by. Worry not, you're in the right place.

Comptons' first rival in those heady days of Old Compton Street's rebirth actually stands on Wardour Street. The Village Soho has also undergone various makeovers and revamps; at the moment it seems to be going through a steel-and-chrome phase (front bar) with a bit of a garden furniture throwback (back bar). It's not hard to see the appeal of the Village – with its two entrances (on Wardour and Brewer Streets) it forms an L-shape, and if you haven't found your friend yet, or indeed if you don't have any friends yet, nothing is easier than walking in one door, pausing among the many modern downlit crannies along the way, and then walking straight out the other door and moving on somewhere else. The Village crowd is younger and more trendy than Comptons, but less so than Rupert Street (see page 2.30) and Freedom. Here too, alcohol exacts a price.

Slightly aloof from the rest of the bars, a little way further north up Wardour Street, is Freedom. This is probably the only Soho gay bar that has a contemporary feel. It's a trendy bar and café with coloured lights and smart decoration. It caters for a swishy 20s crowd and has recently started touting itself as a mixed (gay and straight) bar, so it's worth popping in just to keep the numbers up. If you were in your late teens and still trying to convince the world you were bisexual, you might come here to snog on the sofas. But boozers beware – despite the place's post-modern sexuality its prices are austere. PJ

Old Compton Street

areas

Old Compton Street

OLD COMPTON CAFÉ
ADDRESS 34 Old Compton Street, London W1 (0171–439 3309)
OPEN 24 hours

CLONE ZONE
ADDRESS 64 Old Compton Street, London W1 (0171–287 3530)
OPEN Monday to Saturday, 11.00–21.00; Sunday, 12.00–19.00

BALANS
Address 60 Old Compton Street, London W1 (0171–437 5212)
OPEN Monday to Thursday, 8.00–4.00; Friday and Saturday, 8.00–6.00; Sunday, 8.00–1.00

COMPTONS
ADDRESS 53 Old Compton Street, London W1 (0171–479 7961)
OPEN Monday to Saturday, 12.00–23.00; Sunday, 12.00–22.30

VILLAGE SOHO
ADDRESS 81 Wardour Street, London W1 (0171–434 2124)
OPEN Monday to Saturday, 12.00–1.00; Sunday, 12.00–22.30

FREEDOM
ADDRESS 60–66 Wardour Street, London W1 (0171–734 0071)
OPEN Monday to Saturday, 11.00–3.00; Sunday, 14.00–00.00

UNDERGROUND Leicester Square, Piccadilly Circus, Tottenham Court Road

Old Compton Street

areas

bars and cafés

The Angel	2.2
The Black Cap	2.4
Central Station	2.6
Coleherne	2.8
East End Pubs	2.12
First Out Café	2.22
King William IV	2.24
Royal Vauxhall Tavern	2.26
Rupert Street	2.30
Two Brewers	2.32
The Yard	2.34

The Angel

In the mid-1980s this was the archetypal Islington café/pub. Its brightly coloured and latterly sponged walls screamed left-wing domesticity. It has always had a community feel and the noticeboard has a large number of ads for accommodation, alternative health practitioners, massage, therapy, even one for a barber.

Though increasingly a women's venue (Tuesdays is women-only), there is no lack of men here and no attitude either. The Angel is small, light tables encourage conversation and discourage cruising. This has long been a safe, democratic space, a place where you could bring even the most faint-hearted closet, a place from before the time of AIDS. And it's strange how, once established, a venue's character lingers on, long after the original proprietor has departed, long after the vibe has passed into the mainstream.

Just as the young punks of 1980s Islington have become the movers and shakers of the new media establishment, just as the area has lost some of its buzz, so, with gentrification gathering pace, the ethic of the Angel got on its bike and moved north-east, leaving this pleasant venue behind.

In 1999 redecoration and the opening of the rather cramped basement has seen the venue trying to reinvent itself as a Soho bar with regular DJ and (gasp!) dancing. Whether the new managers have the nerve to overcome our expectations of this old favourite remains to be seen. PJ

ADDRESS 65 Graham Street, London N1 (0171–608 2656)
OPEN daily, 12.00–00.00
MIX lesbian and gay, women-only on Tuesdays
UNDERGROUND Angel

The Angel

bars and cafés

The Black Cap

Judging by the tiled mural just inside the door, The Black Cap has been some kind of hostelry for umpteen years now. It's certainly London's longest-lived gay bar.

Not that you'd know it to look at the place: the latest stage of the ongoing refurbishment programme has left the popular upstairs bar looking like a tart's parlour, with an extensive patio that wouldn't look out of place parked outside an Essex millionaire's passion pad.

'Swish' is the word that comes to mind – and, honey, I don't mean Miss Whiplash.

Downstairs is a long crowded late-night cabaret bar with a regular schedule of strippers and drag acts. You can dance here too, in a crowded kind of way. Camden has little else to offer by way of a gay scene, so people tend to come as part of a crowd and make a night of it … IM

ADDRESS 171 Camden High Street, London NW1 (0171-428 2721)
OPEN Monday to Thursday, 12.00-2.00; Friday and Saturday, 11.00-3.00; Sunday, 12.00-00.00
MIX mainly men
UNDERGROUND Camden Town

The Black Cap

bars and cafés

Central Station

Central Station is one of the few gay pubs in London that actively goes out of its way to support community issues, providing a venue for more than 50 gay and lesbian groups to meet – from HIV and AIDS support organisations to SM dykes – often at no charge to the users. The owners are committed not only to supplying a profit-making entertainment space but to providing a forum where gay issues can be discussed. Recently the Gay and Lesbian Advice Directory (GLAD) was given office space above the pub to carry on its work around gays and the law.

The ground floor consists of a large bar and performance area where there are regular shows, including cabaret, strippers and drag acts of various degrees of polished tediousness and questionable humour. The floor above has a very pleasant café which leads on to a roof terrace bedecked with vines, an ideal place to escape from the steamy depths of the Underground club, which hosts various promotions and a popular disco on Friday and Saturday nights in the low-ceilinged basement bar. Having danced your way through the mass of gyrating bodies, beware the fathomless dark alcoves beyond, where boyfriends have been known to disappear for hours ... WM

ADDRESS 37 Wharfdale Road, London N1 (0171-278 3294)
MIX mainly men
OPEN Monday to Wednesday, 17.00–2.00; Thursday, 17.00–3.00; Friday, 17.00–4.00; Saturday, 12.00–4.00; Sunday, 12.00–00.00
UNDERGROUND King's Cross

Central Station

bars and cafés

Coleherne

The Coleherne has an aura. It has a very heavy reputation as the biggest, oldest, sleaziest leather bar in town. Men (and they are all men) don't just look casually, they stare at you, glare even. It's that old big-daddy thing of 'what have I done wrong?' before you've even done anything. Nowhere will you feel so forcefully that the male thing is one big act, one big show. But what an act, what a show.

It's one huge spectacular of macho posing – like a cartoon silhouette of a man in a black leather jacket and jeans, a T-shirt and large boots. The older regulars here might dress all in leather, the younger ones might wear trainers, but from the jeans-button-style logo to the wipe-clean rubberised floor there are only really three colours at the Coleherne: black, black, and more black.

A good 80 per cent of the customers fall into that vague age group between 30 and 60. So no one is interested in how perfectly you've been keeping yourself – it's more a question of how much you've learned along the way. The atmosphere teeters quite shamelessly between deadly serious and darkest parody.

And that's frankly what makes the Coleherne bearable – its own love of its absurdity. It is self-consciously macho and rightly legendary. When I asked the manager how long the pub had been gay, he cited a 70-year-old regular who'd been coming here for the last 40 years. Age is worn as a burnished bauble, thrust out like a beautiful beer belly, a joy forever. Like all our favourite men, the Coleherne is at ease with itself – accommodating all kinds of male weirdness and sleaze.

In early 1997 the old wooden boards and sawdust were replaced with the current interior of rubber flooring, aluminium, and exposed ventilation shafts. It's still very black, but it's a bit more, well, modern. Upstairs, previously used for private functions, is now a great viewing gallery where

Coleherne

Coleherne

previously used for private functions, is now a great viewing gallery where you can peer down on the main bar or cruise across the drop. The whole place has a good layout – big enough spaces, dark enough in places – and, for such a tightly run operation, a strange sort of freedom. PJ

ADDRESS 261 Brompton Road, London SW5
(0171-244 5951)
OPEN Monday to Saturday, 12.00–23.00;
Sunday, 12.00–22.30
MIX mainly men
UNDERGROUND Earl's Court

Coleherne

bars and cafés

East End Pubs

In direct contrast with the clubs of the West End, the gay pubs of London's East End are friendly, chatty and cheap (in all senses of the word). And the best way to see them is via that traditional English ceremony: the pub crawl. (If you don't understand the etymology of the phrase, just follow our suggested itinerary to its logical conclusion.)

We begin, early one evening, five minutes due north of Liverpool Street station at the Bar, bang next door to Chariots Sauna (see page 7.6). The Bar is not a typical East End pub: it's clean, smart and well-stocked. Indeed, if you get here much before 17.00, you'll have difficulty knowing this is a gay bar: the (straight) owners have an annoying habit of tidying away all gay content during daylight hours, lest they lose the custom of the neighbouring City types and Shoreditch artisans. The Bar is rarely crowded (except on one of the occasional party nights) and the warm summer evenings that bring a chatty crowd to the patio outside are few and far between. Looking around, you wonder whence the cash that supports this lavishness ...

Pondering that, but asking no questions, have a pint of something groovy and foreign here and then walk, while you still can, further north to the church that features in the nursery rhyme ('I'll show that bitch, say the bells of Shoreditch'). Remark, as you pass, the Spiral on the left (of which more later).

Ahead of you stretches Kingsland Road. Another day, if you have time on your hands, take a bus north from here to Abney Park Cemetery (see page 6.2), and watch the languages change on the shopfronts: Hackney has always been a melting pot for successive waves of immigrants, a history of dealing with tribal allegiances that goes some way towards explaining the long tradition of gay pubs in the area.

To your left, beyond the railway bridge, you can see the black mauso-

East End Pubs

bars and cafés

East End Pubs

leum now known as 333 Old Street, but previously the London Apprentice, defunct long enough for everyone to agree that it once was a truly great gay pub. (Needless to say, that wasn't what they said at the time.) Should you wish to explore the trendy straight fleshpots of newly arty Shoreditch (and both the Barley Mow and the Bricklayer's Arms are nice pubs) or if you're here to visit the Ellipsis offices, do that now.

If you're an architecture fan, turn right before the church and coast around Arnold Circus, one of the earliest, and most striking, public-housing estates in London. (I once had spectacular sex on the bandstand here as dawn rose over the rooftops, but alas I cannot guarantee you the same good fortune.)

North-east of Shoreditch Church runs Hackney Road, and Columbia Road branches off to the right. On Sunday mornings this is a busy plant market (see page 9.8) and the Royal Oak (with its special market licence) is a buzzy market pub, where trendy Shoreditch types mingle with gay clubbers who haven't quite got home yet. For the rest of the week, though, this is a quiet street, and a quiet pub, built on traditional (if slightly run-down) lines. There's a dog, a video screen, a pool table. And that's about it. Nonetheless, this is the East End and we must take the rough with the smooth, even in the Pub That Taste Forgot. So have a polite half before moving on.

Several hundred metres north of the Royal Oak, back on the bend of Hackney Road, you should be able to spot the Joiners Arms by its big rainbow flag. Like several other gay pubs on this tour, the Joiners rose out of the ashes of the London Apprentice and on a good night it can be just as busy, just as friendly, and just as difficult to make yourself heard. In common with most other East End venues, the Joiners can occasionally take a while to get going, possibly because it has a growing reputation

East End Pubs

bars and cafés

East End Pubs

for chill-outs that start in the early hours and run through until noon, geared to a mixed gay/straight post-club crowd that (as the title of one chill has it) Can't Stop, Won't Stop. So, assuming this isn't a party night and that you haven't fallen into casual conversation with an off-duty rent boy, a drug-dazed DJ or a drunken dyke, spend this next pint at the Joiners considering how far you've already come from the manicured elegances of the Bar. Just half a mile north and several cultures away already. And it's still early.

When you ask one of the (cute) bar staff to phone you a cab to the Cock and Comfort, don't be dissuaded if he grins and says, 'sod-all cock and precious little comfort'. It's just professional rivalry.

The Cock, half a mile to the south-east, offers another interesting contrast. The predominantly local clientele are a little older and a little more traditional (more than a few of them are refugees from the 'headache-music' at the Joiners). There are no straights, no pool table and no dog. Plus: there's drag.

Time was you couldn't walk into any East End pub, let alone a gay one, without stumbling across some aged drag queen and her ancient routine. ('Don't clap! It's an old building.') But drag, like camp, is a dying art and the Cock and Comfort can pick and choose from among the limited number of stalwart survivors. And, by and large, they choose well.

If you like the Cock, feel free to stay: they're open till 2.00 on Fridays and Saturdays. If you're a very quick drinker, or walker, or crawler, you may still have time to investigate some of the other gay pubs in the neighbourhood: the Old Ship (17 Barnes Street), the British Prince (49 Bromley Street) or the Black Horse (168 Mile End Road).

But if it's a Friday, a Saturday or a Sunday, double back down Bethnal Green Road to the Spiral, a venue which brings new meaning to the term

East End Pubs

bars and cafés

East End Pubs

'dive bar'. (Take the spiral staircase at a run and see what we mean.) Newly redecorated, the Spiral's gutter appeal has suffered from a slight fit of respectability in recent months, an upgrade its dedicated late-night clientele will no doubt redeem in due course: drag queens, market traders, dodgy vicars and terminal sluts – they're all here, and they're all blind drunk.

If, on the other hand, it's a Wednesday, head a mile further south from the Cock to the White Swan on Commercial Road. There may have been a time when burly dockers drank here, but those days have long gone: nowadays it's the standard East End mix of hairdressers and shop assistants, plus a sprinkling of closet yuppies from the nearby Docklands developments lending a little, but not too much, tone. This large and busy pub has a revolving menu of trashy theme nights plus a regular late licence. Wednesday is Amateur Strip Night, its popularity recently boosted by the all-night opening of Sailors Sauna five doors away.

Should you be tempted to get up and show people what you've got, don't let me stop you: you're probably a long way from home and besides no one will remember in the morning. Especially you – now do you see why we call it a pub crawl? IM

THE BAR
ADDRESS Fairchild Street, London EC2 3NS (0171–247 5222)
OPEN Monday to Saturday 11.00–23.00; Sunday 12.00–22.30
UNDERGROUND Liverpool Street

East End Pubs

bars and cafés

East End Pubs

THE ROYAL OAK
ADDRESS 73 Columbia Road, London E2 (0171-739 8204)
OPEN Monday to Saturday, 13.00–late; Sunday, 8.00-22.30
UNDERGROUND Old Street

THE JOINERS ARMS
ADDRESS 116-118 Hackney Road, London E2 (0171-739 9854)
OPEN Monday to Saturday, 12.00-2.00; Sunday, 12.00-22.30
UNDERGROUND Old Street

THE COCK AND COMFORT
ADDRESS 359 Bethnal Green Road, London E2 (0171-729 1090)
OPEN Monday to Thursday, 14.00-23.00; Friday, 14.00-2.00; Saturday, 13.00-2.00; Sunday, 12.00-00.00
UNDERGROUND Bethnal Green

THE SPIRAL
ADDRESS 138 Shoreditch High Street, London E1 (0171-613 1351)
ACCESS varies according to event
OPEN Wednesday to Sunday 22.00-2.00/4.00
UNDERGROUND Liverpool Street

THE WHITE SWAN
ADDRESS 556 Commercial Road, London E1 (0171-780 9870)
OPEN Monday, 21.00-1.00; Tuesday to Thursday, 21.00-2.00; Friday and Saturday, 21.00-3.00; Sunday, 17.30-3.00
UNDERGROUND Aldgate East

East End Pubs

bars and cafés

First Out Café

OK, so you started at the Marble Arch end of Oxford Street, and now you're at Tottenham Court Road. You've been in every clothes shop, you know that shirt was a mistake, you're tired and about to burst into tears. Fear not – what you need is food and drink in a non-oppressive atmosphere. And First Out is just around the corner in St Giles High Street, absolutely in the shadow of Centrepoint.

From the outside, you might think this was a straightforward throwback to the 1970s, and fear wholemeal pasta or worse. But here the pasta doesn't have to be wholemeal, and the salads and cakes are good, as is the coffee. And it's licensed, not just to sell organic wine, but also sensible drinks like whisky and soda. That's just the upstairs part. Downstairs is a likeable small bar where you can drink and smoke without having to eat.

Lurking in the background is an uneasy sense that First Out may any day prove too right on for its own good. Fortunately, however, it hasn't got to that stage yet. What's more, the downstairs bar is one of the few in central London where there's a good chance you'll be able to hear what your desirable table-sharer is saying. Upstairs, it's very much a High Street café – to the extent that it comes as a bit of a shock when you see men kissing each other here. Maybe it's just me, but I think that in London we've come to associate gay life almost exclusively with pubs and clubs, so two men showing affection in a different environment makes one sit up a bit. Damn good thing, too. AW

ADDRESS 52 St Giles High Street, London WC2 (0171–240 8042)
OPEN Monday to Saturday, 10.00–23.00; Sunday 11.00–22.30
MIX lesbian and gay
UNDERGROUND Tottenham Court Road

First Out Café

bars and cafés

King William IV

Everything I know about William IV can be written on the back of a safer-sex shag-me card, but I hardly imagine you'd want to take the trek up to Hampstead just because you're a fan.

If you're in the area already though (and I think we all know why) the William makes a pleasant pit-stop – especially on a warm summer's evening when Heath Street gets quasi-continental.

This is a traditional Hampstead pub: warm, well fitted out and buzzing with relatively intelligent conversation (even on the high days and holidays when the bar staff drag up). There's a pleasant yard out the back in summer and a fire in the front room in winter. The customers could be younger, but so could you, and – excuse me – I didn't notice you being so discerning out on the Heath two hours ago.

Visitors of a monarchist bent may care to couple a visit to the William IV with a trip six stops down the Northern Line to Angel Underground and the King Edward VI – a similar sort of place, but Islington rather than Hampstead, so slightly younger, slightly tattier, and slightly cooler: less corduroy, more designer glasses (see page 1.6).

(Thought for the day: why is no gay bar called The Queen Mary?) IM

ADDRESS 75 Hampstead High Street, London NW3 (0171–435 5747)
OPEN Monday to Saturday, 12.00–23.00; Sunday, 12.00–22.30
MIX mainly men
UNDERGROUND Hampstead

King William IV

bars and cafés

Royal Vauxhall Tavern

The pleasure gardens that once stood at Vauxhall ranked among the greatest attractions in London. For a small fee, the fashionable élite could promenade, picnic and talk among the fragrant, shady bowers. Jonathan Swift visited the gardens to hear the nightingales sing. There were pavilions, music and supper rooms, picturesque ruins and cascades. The grounds were lit with 1000 glass lamps and there were nightly musical entertainments. James Boswell described it as, 'a mixture of curious show – gay exhibition – music, vocal and instrumental, not too refined for the general ear; – for all which only a shilling is paid; and good eating and drinking for those who choose to purchase that regale.'

The large Victorian pub that stands on the site today has been gay for more than 50 years: it was here that many of the old drag stars first trod London boards. And the drag tradition continues here in the south London pleasure garden. Today the Vauxhall doubles as a special-night venue and a regular boozer. Best of the Vauxhall's nights is Saturday's Duckie, where DJs the Reader's Wifes (sic) spin a mixture of old new wave, 1960s lounge, indie and kitsch. But it is the alternative performances that set the agenda, from the gothic drag of the Divine David through the 1970s droll of impressionist Jackie Clune to the vituperative camp rants of Chloe Poems. Why, there's even a stripper with a boa between her legs, and some audience participation. The crowd is about five years either side of 30, fairly beery, and on a good night there's a reasonable male/female mix. The acts themselves can be quite cool: you're unlikely to feel embarrassed, though you might whoop a bit and learn to laugh a little at the foibles of the gay crowd.

In addition to Duckie, the Vauxhall's biggest night, there is also Youthclub on Tuesdays ('50 years of pop culture'); Wednesday is Wig 'n' Casino, a northern soul night; Thursday is cabaret; Friday is Vixens, women-only

Royal Vauxhall Tavern

bars and cafés

Royal Vauxhall Tavern

night; Sundays is cabaret from 12.00 to 16.00 and from 21.00 there's a chill-out night playing 'classic Love Muscle anthems'.

A venue, as Boswell wrote of the Vauxhall Gardens, 'peculiarly adapted to the taste of the English nation'. PJ

ADDRESS 372 Kennington Lane, London SE11 (0171–582 0833)
OPEN Monday to Thursday, 21.00–1.00; Friday (women-only) and Saturday, 21.00–2.00; Sunday, 12.00–22.30
MIX lesbian and gay
UNDERGROUND Vauxhall

Royal Vauxhall Tavern

bars and cafés

Rupert Street

For many gay men and women, Rupert Street is to bars what Rupert Murdoch is to newspapers: this is the gay flagship of Bass Taverns, whose ruthless corporate pursuit of the pink pound through a series of high-profile homo haunts has alienated many, and whose monopoly on the beer tents at Gay Pride (see page 12.2) – and the high prices charged there – have alienated even more.

Like it or not, though, queens have always had a thing for flags and ships (especially if the barmen are cute and the toilets are clean), and Rupert Street is rarely less than busy. And, who knows, some may even find the idea of drinking behind big plate-glass windows in a brightly lit bar on a busy Soho street strangely… liberating.

If, on the other hand, you want your queer culture unassimilated and non-homogenised, cool rather than 'trendy', take your custom around the corner to Bar Code in Archer Street: better music, better beer and, believe me, better men. IM

ADDRESS 50 Rupert Street, London W1 (0171–292 7141)
OPEN Monday to Saturday, 12.00–23.00; Sunday, 12.00–22.30
MIX lesbian and gay
UNDERGROUND Piccadilly Circus

Rupert Street

bars and cafés

Two Brewers

The front bar of this longstanding south London venue is done out like a cinema foyer, with fussy curves, railings and the late 1980s lighting of the generic Soho bar. The walls have cartoony acrylic portraits of drag stars. A back door opens on to a larger, black-painted dance area with a long busy bar. This part is the stuff of large provincial towns with one gay bar that caters for all. There is a well-sprung dancefloor, no seats, a large video screen, very loud music and acoustics bad enough to make your ears bleed. If you stand still at a certain point on the dancefloor (just the other side of the small dividing wall, left side) you feel the strange combination of static and vibration lift the hair on the top of your head.

The music is poppy house, chart stuff and some old disco. Ultraviolet and flickering lights attempt to create depth and contrast in an otherwise shallow space. The result is an irritating jumble of vibrating light patches, and a sickly sense of disorientation.

Despite the obvious effort and expense of the recent refit, you'd have to be ten pints under to experience any sense of euphoria in this place. The crowd is easy going enough, an unpretentious mixture of queens and blokiness, herded in and out, fed gassy beer, and bashed with the aural handbag. It remains to be seen whether they can do anything with this frankly hostile space. Though since it's Clapham's only large gay venue, it has a better chance than most. PJ

ADDRESS 114 Clapham High Street, SW4 (0171-498 4971)
OPEN Monday to Thursday, 12.00–2.00; Friday and Saturday, 12.00–3.00; Sunday, 12.00–00.00
MIX lesbian and gay
ACCESS £2 after 22.00 Friday and Saturday, otherwise free
UNDERGROUND Clapham Common

Two Brewers

bars and cafés

The Yard

The Yard was one of the earliest colonial stakeouts in what has now become a busy Boystown centred on Old Compton Street (see page 1.12). Consequently it's cornered what has got to be one of the nicest pieces of property in the area.

A long narrow alley (just difficult enough to find to make the hunt worthwhile) debouches into an airy courtyard with a dull downstairs bar and an iron stairs-and-balcony combo that leads up to a pleasantly sophisticated loft-style first-floor lounge. The courtyard itself is only practical for drinking in at the height of summer, and the upstairs bar has restricted opening hours, largely thanks to the local residents' constant rear-guard battle to minimise noisy numbers. So, until recently at least, the Yard has rather failed to live up to its early promise.

All this will change later in 1999, when the Yard plans to enfold its whole space within a glass dome. This will inevitably mean it will be closed for a while – but there are at least eight other gay venues within staggering distance, so pop by and hope to find it open. IM

ADDRESS 57 Rupert Street, London W1 (0171-437 2652)
OPEN Monday to Saturday, 12.00–23.00; Sunday, 12.00–22.30
MIX lesbian and gay
UNDERGROUND Piccadilly Circus

The Yard

bars and cafés

clubs

Backstreet	3.2
Benjy's 2000	3.4
The Block	3.6
Club Kali	3.8
Club V	3.10
DTPM	3.12
GAY	3.14
Heaven	3.18
Popstarz	3.22
Substation South	3.26
Trade	3.30

Backstreet

Legend has it that a dragon with a bad attitude and a nasty tongue guards Backstreet's firmly closed doors, and Lord only knows what goes on behind them: me, I don't do leather, never have, never will – and besides, our budget didn't stretch to a new outfit. From what I hear, though, if you just want to try life a tad transgressive, or find yourself fancying a pop at a pill-fuelled weekend of whippery-zippery, this is not the bar for you. Find out where Suzie Kruger is holding FIST this month and shell out on that: she stays open much later, and she's a little less masterful in her definition of 'strict dress code'.

On the other hand, if you're remotely serious about the leather scene you probably know all about this place already, and will have packed your bags accordingly: it is, after all, London's last proud gasp from a serious fetish scene that's being date-stamped to death by eagle-eyed marketing men in suits all over Europe. Plus, presumably, you'll know a good proportion of the clientele. Backstreet holds well over 100 people on a good night, so the chances are high that you'll bump into that blond from Berlin with the pierced lip and the Prince Albert who left you tied to his rafters for six hours while he went out to the opera.

But don't confuse Backstreet with Benjy's (see page 3.4), even though they're only yards apart – full zipper mask and black leather harness is not a good look in a room full of East End boy-babes, trust me. IM

ADDRESS Wentworth Mews, off Burdett Road, London E3 (0181-980 8557)
OPEN Thursday to Saturday, 22.00–3.00; Sunday, 21.00–2.00
MIX men-only
ACCESS Thursday and Sunday £2.50; Friday and Saturday £3
UNDERGROUND Mile End

Backstreet

clubs

Benjy's 2000

Did you see *The Last Days of Disco*? That long tracking-shot where they walk through the doors, up the stairs and into the room like Reservoir Puppies, up into the light, the heat, the noise – and then start dancing around their handbags? Benjy's 2000, as its name implies, is very like that: very 1980s, very disco. Rather cheesy.

As it happens, the name derives from the Jewish entrepreneur who carved the place out of an old cinema, and whose widow now runs it as an entirely straight venue for the rest of the week. But hey, every other cute Essex boy you see here on a Sunday might as well be called Benjy. Or Marcus. Or Steve.

The joke about Benjy's used to be that this was the place to come if you wanted to know what was going cheap down the market next week. But the markets, and the boys, have moved on since then – the kids have discovered chemicals, and the average Benjy's crowd has aged slightly as a result.

But despite an early close (1.00? oh please) and the startlingly high beer prices, Benjy's makes a good way to end a relatively low-octane weekend: marvel at the campy decor, gasp at the brightly lit toilets, squint at the twinkly lights, avoid yourself in any one of a thousand mirrors and … dance, dance, dance. (And then catch a cab to the Spiral in Shoreditch High Street and drink, drink, drink.) IM

ADDRESS 562A Mile End Road, London E3 (0181–980 6427)
OPEN Sunday, 21.00–1.00 (last admission 24.00)
MIX lesbian and gay
ACCESS £2
UNDERGROUND Mile End

Benjy's 2000

clubs

The Block

You can picture the scene: two floors of black paint, with very little light and a lot of camouflage netting, military semiotics on the walls, a pool table here, a darkroom there. A couple of small bars. And a constant eddy of horny hunters, cruising backwards and forwards, looking you up and down, every man his own porn star. (You can't picture the scene? Put this book down immediately; you're straight.)

I've only managed to get out to the Block a few times, so I can't tell how many people here know each other already. Quite a few, I suspect, given that the denim/uniform/skinhead dress-code crowd don't have many places left to go at the moment. Which is not, of course, to say that they engage in much conversation: the odd muttered reference to an unadmitted case of the clap, or a polite enquiry about T-cell counts just about covers it. These boots weren't made for walking, and these mouths aren't meant for talking …

Dress butch and go, especially at the weekend (or dress anyhow and check out Underworld). There's an excellent mini-cab service to get you back to civilisation, the music's not bosch-bosch-bosch and, who knows, you might even meet someone. (Tip: I'll be the one drinking beer in a bottle so I can stick it in my pocket and have both hands free.) IM

ADDRESS 28 Hancock Road, London E3 (0181–988 0257)
OPEN Wednesday (Underworld), Thursday and Sunday 22.00–3.00; Friday and Saturday, 22.00–6.00
MIX men-only
ACCESS Wednesday, £3; Thursday and Sunday, £3 members/£4 guests; Friday and Saturday, £5 members/£6 guests
UNDERGROUND Bromley-by-Bow

The Block

clubs

Club Kali

This is one of the best dance nights in London, attracting a crowd bused in from all over the country whose enjoyment of the eclectic mix of Bhangra, Hindi, house and Arabic music spun by DJs Ritu and Rizwan is contagious. The sight of electric-blue, indigo and gold saris, crimson wedding waistcoats and Doc Martens swirling across the floor to the latest sounds from Egypt, Morocco and India mixed with Bhangra Muffin from Birmingham is exhilarating.

The middle of the dancefloor is dominated by the 'Chutney Queens', who imitate the song-and-dance routines of their favourite Hindi film-stars. 'Don't be deceived by their coyness – they're reptiles in peacocks' feathers,' said Ishmal from Wolverhampton, a former teacher of Islamic studies. Clips from classic Bollywood movies are projected from a large screen suspended from the ceiling; around the edge of the dancefloor are small tables with bowls of fruit.

One of the warmest, most attitude-free clubs in the city. WM

ADDRESS The Dome, 1 Dartmouth Park Hill, London N19
OPEN monthly on third Friday, 22.00–3.00
MIX lesbian and gay
ACCESS £5/£3 concessions before 23.00; £6/£4 concessions after
UNDERGROUND Tufnell Park

Club Kali

clubs

Club V

Resolutely small scale and now an established part of Hackney and Islington's alternative scene, this fortnightly bash is one of the most individual. Unlike Popstarz (see page 3.22), which has moved from venue to venue but kept more or less the same music, Club V has declined opportunities to move to a larger space, saving experimentation for the playlist. In a reflection of indie's do-it-yourself culture, the club is run by the four founding DJs. While bar profits go to the Mean Fiddler, monies from the door pay for booking bands and extending the vast collection of musical alternatives.

Popular with those who'd rather drink beer and pogo than show off their pecs, this is one of the few nights on the scene where the two sexes actually talk to one another. As a result, neither dominates. The many regulars and the informality of the DJs – playing requests and dancing themselves – create an unpretentious atmosphere. The decor is simple: a long black room with a stage at one end where bands play early in the evening. Huge photocopies of alternative queers bedeck the black walls and a scattering of tables and chairs around the small dancefloor gives the room the feel of a student social. When quiet, it can seem overwhelmingly earnest, but on a good night Club V can seem the friendliest place on the scene. A real alternative. PJ

ADDRESS upstairs at The Garage, 20–22 Highbury Corner, London N1 (0171–607 1818)
OPEN fortnightly on second and fourth Saturday, 20.30–2.00
MIX lesbian and gay
ACCESS £3.50/£2.50 with flyer/£2 concessions
UNDERGROUND Highbury & Islington

Club V

clubs

DTPM

3.12

The interior of The End is bright, cool and crisp. There are large dance spaces, nice curved sofas to lounge on, fine air conditioning and a sound system to die for.

DTPM is the most established Sunday gay chill-out. The music is loud but the acoustics are so good you can still hear your partner talking.

The crowd is young, relaxed, muscly and loved-up. You see a lot of rubberised fabrics, short-sleeved shirts, turn-ups and state-of-the-art trainers. You feel a controlled, deferred euphoria. Like a cool, slow burning at the back of your head. In the bathroom a man hands you a paper towel in case your hands are shaking too much. PJ

ADDRESS The End, 16 West Central Street, London WC1
(0171-419 9199)
OPEN Sunday, 20.00-4.00
MIX lesbian and gay
ACCESS £10
UNDERGROUND Tottenham Court Road

DTPM

clubs

GAY

There's a line of exhibitionists on stage, some with shirts on, some without, boys from the suburbs who do the whole routine every night in front of the mirror, a row of teenage testosterone waiting to burst. They look out across the dancefloor below, point their fingers at the people dancing and smile huge broad grins, working themselves into a frenzy. Farther up, mid circle, there's a moment of panic in planet control as one of the large balloons gets loose and strays over the vast mixing desk. But nothing ever stops here, nothing interrupts the operation. And it's a very slick operation too: discreet but firm security, air conditioning on full throttle, and the queues move fast because everyone wants to start enjoying themselves right away. The boys here keep walking, keep talking, back over their shoulders. It's not the beat from the drugs even, it's not that fast, it's the beat of being slightly overexcited on a Saturday night. Over 2000 of them coming up, London's biggest gay night, more choice than you'll ever need.

And what choice. People still vogue here, people do modern dance steps, people have complete routines: 'I travel the world and the (count them) seven seas.' Everyone's dressed as though they're going on a holiday in the Med ('everyone's looking for something'), though with its garish colours and clean, fresh tastelessness, this could be anywhere in Europe. A pair of denim cut-offs sashays past and it's still January.

The hour before 1.00 it builds and it builds, and we're going higher, higher, we're slightly tipsy, slightly dizzy, with the embarrassed smiles of people who feel they might be enjoying, might be making fools of, themselves. Ooh, ooh, it's all so UNPRETENTIOUS! Here comes George, here comes Frankie, here comes the 1980s bloody megamix. Not everyone has a routine to 'Diva' yet, but they give it a go (Cliiiioopaaahh-htraaaahhh!!!!). And at some point a collective euphoria kicks in, you

GAY

clubs

GAY

can't help but smile. Just as your irony surfaces, you find you're laughing all over yourself. It's intoxicatingly silly.

At about 1.00 there's an act on stage, usually cheesy or a camp has-been. Come 1.30 there's a frenzied hopping and chewing going on upstairs; up in the gallery of the main circle there's a blur of leaning bodies but no space to sit down, and no time. Out back, male shrieking comes from the ladies' toilet.

Of the places I visited, this was the one where absolutely everyone seemed to be having a good time. It's absolutely big business, it's absolutely organised and the music sucks. But it surely delivers. All of us, everybody's been. Raining Men anyone? PJ

ADDRESS The Astoria, 157 Charing Cross Road, London WC2
(0171-734 6963)
OPEN Saturday, 22.30-5.00
MIX lesbian and gay
ACCESS £10
UNDERGROUND Tottenham Court Road

GAY

clubs

Heaven

Opened in the late 1970s, for a long time Heaven was so disproportionately big it could afford to see off all rivals. The club offered more choice: from the beginning it had several different levels playing different music and attracting different crowds. In the world of Saturday-night gay cruising, the more choice you have, the better your chances of picking up and the better your evening will be. Heaven had high currency indeed. It was, and still is, so well known internationally – often the only place people know of in London – and so centrally placed it could pull in the whole tourist crowd and still fill up with locals on a rainy weekday night. It made a virtue of reliability. You always knew what it would be like and you knew it would always be packed. It was the gay club. Even straights had heard of it.

The club went through a variety of transformations in the late 1970s and 1980s, and while it seemed occasionally to lose its direction, it could always guarantee a crowd. Things began to change with the arrival of the Fridge's Saturday nighters. Then in the mid 1990s Jeremy Joseph's GAY (see page 3.14) declared itself London's biggest gay night. In terms of pure numbers Heaven had lost.

In 1998 the club was shut for six months and extensively refurbished. Considerable changes have not destroyed the character of the place. There is still the long tunnel of arches, now painted red and with a long bar. There is still the cavernous brick barn of the dancefloor, though the viewing gallery has been lowered and the sound system improved. Upstairs (the 'starbar') two smaller bars stand at either end of a large central dancefloor. The service is still abysmal, the staff sloppy and seemingly slightly oppressed.

Heaven's reputation has meant that over the years it has been able to get away with more or less anything: a lot of attitude, inflated prices and

Heaven

clubs

Heaven

some really duff midweekers. It never convincingly succeeds with alternative nights, it's too mainstream. It's best when it sticks to the basic formula: big, cruisy, upbeat Friday and Saturday nights. It's a peculiarly public space, a place to put yourself on show. And the venue is so vast the different types counteract one another and enforce a general code of behaviour.

There are hints of corporate control in the club itself (it is after all owned by, and responsible to, Virgin). So you'll find yourself and another half dozen bemused punters waiting ten minutes to be served while the anxious barboy mops down the bar. Somehow you know he's been told to keep all his surfaces clean. It's company policy. Of all the clubs we visited, this was the only one that refused to sanction free photography. It was company policy, we were told. As in many public spaces a strange form of control exists at Heaven, a control at times so palpable it might make you decide to stay away. And it's a blessing of living in London at the present time that this is no longer the best the scene has to offer. There are alternatives, both larger and smaller. And after all we've been through together, it's a blessing to know we don't have to do this any more. PJ

ADDRESS under The Arches, Villiers Street, London WC2 (0171-930 2020)
OPEN Monday (Popcorn) and Wednesday (Fruit Machine), 22.30-3.00; Friday (Wildlife), 22.30-6.00; Saturday, 22.30-5.00
MIX Saturday: lesbian and gay; Monday, Wednesday and Friday: lesbian and gay/straight
ACCESS Monday £3/£1 with flyer/free NUS; Wednesday £6/£4 with flyer/£1 with flyer before 23.30; Friday £8/£4 NUS; Saturday £10
UNDERGROUND Charing Cross

Heaven

clubs

Popstarz

It's still all here – the Madchester fishing hats, the turn-ups, the satin patterned shirts. Drink beer from a can. It's 00.35 and they're playing 'She Bangs the Drum' on the main indie floor, while out in the corridor it feels like the early stages of a good sixth-form house party. You pass the same indecisive boys, deciding eventually to dance.

When this place opened on a Sunday night in 1995 it attracted a dissolute bunch of arty students and wannabes. Riding on the crest of Britpop, before the bad Blur album, just around the time of 'Common People', it was indie and pop and retro new wave and beer, when you couldn't drink beer because you were supposed to be popping pills, taking your shirt off and having a lifestyle. All at once you didn't need a lifestyle. You could see the relief on the punters' faces. Nice men with real personalities smiled at you and took you home. It was as if all the normal people had suddenly decided to go out on the same night.

Popstarz got bigger and moved to a Saturday. Having started at the Paradise (as The Complex was then known), it moved to Bagleys and became huge, then thinned out and moved to the Hanover Grand. Then it took up residence at the Leisure Lounge in Holborn. At some point it moved to a Friday night. Then in the first weeks of 1999 it moved back to The Complex.

And somewhere along the line Popstarz changed. While it once broke open the scene, no one could now pretend it's still breaking down any barriers. The venue is twice as large as it once was, with big beat, indie, trash and Motown on consecutive floors. The new layout is part exciting, part annoying, the last two floors being reached by a narrow staircase where bouncers shout at you to keep moving. It's a pity, because despite the hackneyed disco played up there, the top floor is really the best. With its cushioned walls of red plastic, tented ceiling and low tables lit up from

Popstarz

clubs

Popstarz

from below, it feels like a womb-like cocktail lounge. Some way from the original indie kids, but light years from the dreary Heaven revamp (see page 3.18).

One last caveat. For a club that prides itself so much on its alcohol consumption, ordering a drink here is abysmally slow. Drink from a can? Forget it, bring a flask. PJ

ADDRESS The Complex, Parkfield Street, London N1 (0171–738 2336)
OPEN Friday, 22.00–5.00
MIX lesbian and gay/straight
ACCESS £7/£4 concessions/£6 with flyer/£5 with flyer before 23.00
UNDERGROUND Angel

Popstarz

clubs

Substation South

Wayne Shires' Substation empire staked its initial claim on the West End in Falconberg Court, just behind GAY (see page 3.14) on Charing Cross Road. It was here that the prototypical Substation mix first gelled: industrial decor, undemanding music, rotating theme nights.

From Falconberg Court the empire expanded south of the river to Brixton, with Substation South. At much the same time Substation Soho, as it was now known, moved into roomier premises on the other side of Soho Square (whence it has only recently departed to take up residence at the Soundshaft, behind Heaven – see page 3.18).

When Substation South first opened, success seemed less than certain. Although gay people, with their traditional penchant for colonising largely immigrant areas, had already become a visible part of Brixton's much-touted cultural diversity, those who didn't actually live there still had alarming memories of the riots and muggings that were part of the folklore of the 1980s.

Nonetheless, Substation South has survived and prospered, offering a carefully modulated menu of theme nights with a raunchy edge. Some nights are sexier than others: Queer Nation, now established here in a regular Saturday-night slot, is notable for having carved out a large and loyal following on the basis of its music policy and ethnic mix alone. (It does no harm that the only other club nights offering a soul and garage mix can currently be counted on the fingers of one hand.)

But now that Love Muscle at the nearby Fridge has closed, Brixton's credentials as a place worth the trek across town look increasingly thin: unlike nearby Clapham, or Vauxhall, there has never been a gay pub in this area, for instance.

If you're staying somewhere with good connections to Brixton underground, then certainly give Substation South a try during the week (the

Substation South

clubs

Substation South

in-house gay cab firm, Battersea's Q Cars, will get you home in good company at a fair price). Otherwise, unless you really are a dedicated techno fan, or want to give the Y-Front underwear night a try (see page 12.6), save your visit for a Saturday. IM

ADDRESS 9 Brighton Terrace, London SW9 (0171–737 2095)
OPEN Monday (Y-Front), 22.00–3.00; Tuesday and Thursday (Toolbox), 21.30–2.00; Wednesday (Absolutely), 21.30–3.00; Friday (Dirty Dishes), 22.00–5.00; Saturday, 22.30–5.00; Sunday, 21.00–3.00
MIX Monday, Tuesday and Thursday men-only; otherwise lesbian and gay
ACCESS Monday to Thursday free before 23.00, Monday and Wednesday £3, Tuesday and Thursday £2; Friday £4; Saturday £6 or £7 depending on event
UNDERGROUND Brixton

Substation South

clubs

Trade

It's red in here, is it the lighting? It feels moist: the air's humid, and everything and everyone vibrates. Ventilation shafts loom up from the floor like on the deck of a liner, knobbled like the folded tentacles of an octopus, lurking down here. As though at any moment the floor might buckle and everyone be thrown up in a mish-mash of surf, hands waving, a thrashing of tentacles, suckers hanging off the walls. Bodies pass, brushing off their wetness. Great chests and arms, bodies two or three deep line the wall, a moist, humanly padded corridor. Strange fish glance this way and that, flick their tails and are gone. Large cold drops of water fall from the ceiling. It's the bottom of some underwater world, an absurd urban aquarium.

And off here and off there, two dancefloors, so packed and monotonous with muscle moving. Two bars, downlit. Green laser light flickers across a monstrous sea of heads. And it's loud-loud, loud-loud, loud-loud, music so mindless, it's hardly here. Feel the beats' dull thud break across the back of your neck. Or ignore it. Noise, noise, hanging unheard in the drug-fuddled fusion that surrounds you.

Saturday night/Sunday morning, Trade is the main event. If you're going to do this London gay-scene thing, you may as well do it properly. And Trade fairly much does the whole thing. PJ

ADDRESS Turnmills, 63B Clerkenwell Street, London EC1 (0171–250 3409)
MIX lesbian and gay/straight
ACCESS annual membership £25; admission £10 members/£15 non-members and guests
OPEN Sunday, 4.00–13.00
UNDERGROUND Farringdon

Trade

clubs

hotels and restaurants

Balans West 4.2
Philbeach and New York Hotels 4.6
No 7 Guesthouse 4.10
The Peasant 4.12

Balans West

Located on the corner where Earl's Court Road crosses the Old Brompton Road, Balans West occupies a prime site at the head of Earl's Court's gay stretch. Less frantic than its big brother on Old Compton Street (see page 1.12), this brightly decorated, gay-friendly restaurant attracts a smart thirtysomething crowd and there's none of the politics and vegetarianism you find at First Out (see page 2.22).

The menu is best described as Californian with Mediterranean influences and the food is self-consciously nouvelle. Starters are priced from £3.50 to £4.50 and salads range from a modest Tomato Salad (£3.35) to Warm Szechuan Chicken at £5.25. Mains come in at between £5.95 for a Leek and Sweet Potato Charlotte and £10.95 for Goan Fish Curry. There's a broad selection of wines, cocktails and beers. Pitchers of cocktails are available at £12.50 a time.

Despite Balans' high aspirations I found the atmosphere self-conscious and the food unconvincing. The mustard walls, blue tables and terracotta and aquamarine seating don't exactly help. You eat perfectly well here, but somehow character seems to have been forfeited in favour of presentation. A note on the menu reads, 'Please no pipes, cigars or herbal cigarettes' – a little baffling as the air was unpleasantly smoky. There are a lot of waiters and the service is extremely fast and efficient, though I had the feeling that they were all rather miserable about something.

Somehow I wanted something more from the place. A little more character, a little more chutzpah and a little more individuality in the cooking. Having said that, one should welcome the diversification of gay businesses, and Balans does provide a pleasant venue for the lifestyle-conscious young queen.

It's an OK place to have breakfast or lunch too – especially if you grab

Balans West

hotels and restaurants

Balans West

a table in the light-filled, metal-framed conservatory towards the rear of the restaurant, which looks out on to a wall topped with pot plants.

If you prefer more traditional food and like infiltrating the straight world and turning it queer, however, you might prefer to try the Troubadour Coffee House a few doors down. PJ

ADDRESS 239 Old Brompton Road, London SW5 (0171-244 8838)
MIX lesbian and gay
OPEN Monday to Saturday, 8.00–1.00
UNDERGROUND Earl's Court

Balans West

hotels and restaurants

Philbeach and New York Hotels

Half way around Philbeach Gardens, just before the white-fronted crescent turns to red brick, the Philbeach Hotel spreads its awning. The entrance seems grandly promising enough and the reception area appears to have all its hardwood surrounds in place. But the decor is incongruous. The main areas are plastered with heavy masculine stripes, and ugly chandeliers cast a harsh, critical light. The lounge is strangely unnerving – more garish stripes and some Timney Fowler friezes give it a pompous, slightly late-1980s feel, bleached-blond Americans lounge on the sofas, and in a frame in the corner the ex-Princess of Wales looks coyly down, as though this were vulgarity too much even for her.

Passing through the hallway you come to the garden restaurant, Wilde About Oscar. The walls are decked out in a trellis pattern and the ceiling has cloth roses dotted along arching lines. Two walls of the restaurant look out on to a terrace and a small garden, which is lit at night. The food is standard modern French/European fare; the menu changes every three months. Starters are around £4, mains between £10 and £12, desserts £4 average. There's little for vegetarians – the omelette, perhaps. Given the restaurant's middle-aged clientele, the dance music and the strangely nervous waiters can be a little jarring, though the former changes to show-tunes later on.

There are 40 rooms, half doubles, half singles, ranging from the comfortable to the frankly box-like. The hotel tries to give an impression of classic English decor, antiques and good taste, but too many rooms have been divided and decorated cheaply, so the corridors and doors are ugly and faintly institutional, the wallpaper a mish-mash.

The hotel has existed for 20 years, the restaurant for five, and clearly has a loyal clientele. The owners sold a similar venture in Edinburgh to finance the refurbishment of the downstairs bar, the decoration of which

hotels and restaurants

Philbeach and New York Hotels

is a pleasant surprise after the rest. Painted in orange and blue, this bright and roomy space gives out on to a plain patio area. There are more pictures of Diana here and more showtunes. There is also a regular TV/TS night, Lipstick, on every second Monday, where clients can change for dinner and have the run of the downstairs bar.

The place clearly caters to an American guest's view of England and English hospitality. But the overall impression is of people ill at ease with themselves and the place left me wishing it had been a little *less* gay.

Next door to the Philbeach is the New York Hotel, open since 1991 and clearly a product of the Philbeach's success. However, this younger sister is less pretentious, more friendly, less anxious about its status – and unlike the Philbeach, it looks as though it's been decorated in one piece. Though smaller than its neighbour (18 rooms in all) and providing only breakfast in the dining room, it looks more like a hotel, more professional and so strangely more welcoming. There is the odd chandelier here too – and a Jacuzzi – but the rooms are more pleasant and you could easily ignore the odd statue if you had a mind to. PJ

PHILBEACH HOTEL
ADDRESS 30–31 Philbeach Gardens, London SW5 (0171-373 1244)
ACCESS singles £35–£55; doubles/triples £58–£85
OPEN Wilde About Oscar daily 19.00–22.30

NEW YORK HOTEL
ADDRESS 32 Philbeach Gardens, London SW5 (0171-244 6884)
ACCESS singles £50–£55; doubles/triples £70–£110

UNDERGROUND Earl's Court

Philbeach and New York Hotels

hotels and restaurants

No 7 Guesthouse

This modest but pleasant guesthouse stands amid a crescent of trees, about ten minutes walk from Brixton Underground. It has eight good-sized rooms, all with private bathroom, colour TV, telephone and fridge, some with air conditioning and original fireplaces. No main meals are served, but there's a breakfast room looking on to a small pleasant garden. Paul and John, the couple who run the hotel, were property developers in the area before setting up here in 1992, so the house is a veritable minefield of ingenious home improvements.

There is a bronze David on one of the staircases, but on the whole the decor is uncluttered, avoiding campiness in favour of simple comfort. The couple seem relaxed about their own sexuality, and extend an accepting and supportive welcome to those still in the closet. The clientele includes all ages and Paul and John stress that they expect guests to respect each other's privacy. The hotel does 80 per cent of its trade with foreign tourists, and 80 per cent of those are North American. As no one comes to London for the weather, it's busy all year round. It's advisable to book about a month in advance, though you could be lucky with a late cancellation. PJ

ADDRESS 7 Josephine Avenue, London SW2 (0181–674 1880)
WEBSITE http://www.no7.com
MIX lesbian and gay
ACCESS rooms from £49 to £89 per night
UNDERGROUND Brixton

No 7 Guesthouse

hotels and restaurants

The Peasant

The Peasant is gay-owned, but it doesn't depend on blanket support from the community for its success – it's the quality of the food and the excellent service provided by the very attractive staff that maintain its reputation.

On the ground floor, in what would once have been the public bar of this large Victorian former pub, tables are set for lunch or dinner in a bright, surprisingly modern setting. The walls, once deep lavender and now a warm ochre, form an effective contrast with the nineteenth-century mosaic flooring. This is a wonderful place to sit in the early evening, when the light floods through the huge curved windows, sipping a glass of wine or excellent beer and chewing on an olive.

On the first floor, reached by a heavy mahogany staircase, is the main restaurant, a beautiful open space with windows on three sides and an exotically planted roof terrace. Finely carved masks decorate the white walls and pedestals supporting contemporary sculpture divide the space.

The menu – modern British with Pacific Rim influences – is available on both floors and is changed every two months: the monk fish and mashed potato is strongly recommended. Main courses come in at around £10; the wine list offers a catholic choice of European and New World wines. WM

ADDRESS Room 240 at the Peasant, 240 St John Street, London EC1 (0171-336 7726)
OPEN lunch, 12.30–15.00; dinner, 18.30–23.00
MIX lesbian and gay/straight
UNDERGROUND Angel

The Peasant

hotels and restaurants

en plein air

Chelsea Physic Garden	**5.2**
City Churches	**5.6**
Kew Gardens	**5.18**
Thames Boat Trip	**5.22**

Chelsea Physic Garden

Chelsea's generally pleasant image is belied by all of the approach routes to the Physic Garden.

Go via the King's Road and you have to contend with robotic unemployed shoppers followed by the Thatcherite ghosts which gibber and squeak their way along Flood Street. Take the Royal Hospital Road approach, and it's just rather dreary: low, unpleasing buildings (some complete with peculiar old men in red coats) and wide unpleasing spaces – the one high spot is a quite beautiful demure deco/moderne block of flats. And walking along the Embankment, notwithstanding the fine views over the river, is far too much like walking along the hard shoulder of a motorway (yes, I have, actually) for comfort. So the Physic Garden has a lot to transcend, which it duly does.

Entered via a discreet doorway and concealed for the most part behind high brick walls, this is emphatically not a place to bring a dog, child, ball or frisbee, thank god. It remains the working garden it has been for more than 300 years, and the sense of privilege at being allowed in, the feeling of being admitted on sufferance, is reinforced by the extremely restricted opening hours, the no-nonsense straightness of the paths and the unlyrical labelling of the plants.

Although not as old as its counterpart in Oxford, the garden is of some historical importance, having been a source of plants and seeds for botanic gardens around the world since its foundation in the 1670s. It was also the supplier of the seed which provided the roots, so to speak, of the North American cotton industry.

But perhaps this is an unnecessarily austere picture: there is a wonderful peacefulness about the place, paradoxically combined with a sense of purpose, which adds a quality missing from most public gardens. Quite how it is that brick walls, beds of humus and restrained explosions

Chelsea Physic Garden

en plein air

Chelsea Physic Garden

of trees and other plants manage to convey a sense of cared-forness and expertise, I don't know. But they do.

Again, though, this is hardly the place to take a picnic. So have lunch before you go, and then take tea afterwards in one of the cafés around Sloane Square. AW

ADDRESS 66 Royal Hospital Road, London SW3 (0171-352 5646)
OPEN April to October: Wednesday, 12.00–17.00; Sunday, 14.00–18.00
ACCESS £3.50; £1.80 children and concessions
UNDERGROUND Sloane Square

Chelsea Physic Garden

en plein air

City Churches

Try an east-to-west walk, starting at Spitalfields and ending at St Paul's.

Christ Church Spitalfields is an outrageous building – take the tower: high, but heavy and dominant. Nicholas Hawksmoor (1661–1736), architect of some of London's most remarkable baroque churches, takes Sir Christopher Wren (1632–1723) as his starting point and then tries to go further. The interior is dominated by the weight of grey stone. It feels as though the building is higher than it is long or broad, but this is an illusion generated by the eye being drawn upwards by the carved barrel vaults above the side aisles, the coffered ceiling above the nave, and inescapably the massive stone beam which carries the royal coat of arms. (As a matter of fact, the eye would do almost anything to avoid engaging with the tatty chairs at ground level.) The church has been in the midst of a multi-million pound restoration programme for years, and this is set to continue for more years. At the time of writing, the impact of the building work is such that opening hours are restricted (it claims to be open from 12.00 to about 14.00 every day, but this is often not the case) so the best way of seeing inside may be to go to one of the concerts in the summer or winter music festivals (see page 11.26).

Down Commercial Street, which sits oddly on the cusp of Bangladeshi rag-trade poverty and City money, to Aldgate – a hell of 1960s brutalist architecture, traffic and confusing pedestrian underpasses. And so to St Botolph's, Aldgate (1741–44), whose interior is the product of a species of evangelical Christian colour blindness. The building isn't much rated by architectural historians, but the broad gallery running round the squarish interior is very pleasing. If only someone would fire-bomb the disgusting Victorian stained glass of the east window and the 1970s batik work in contrasting shades of pink – well-meaning evangelo-art at its nadir. However, the main reason for coming here is the role of this church

City Churches

en plein air

City Churches

in gay history. It was the centre of the gay Christian movement through the 1970s and 1980s, until the fascist wing of the Church of England gained the ascendancy locally and turfed out the queens, thus leading unerringly to the attention-seeking Peter Tatchell some years later committing outrage on the Archbishop of Canterbury in his very own pulpit. The reliquaries are stuffed with bullet-scarred metatarsi …

Leaving the church, turn right, and you will wonder if you accidentally dropped a tab of acid at breakfast. On the skyline, hoisted a good 30 metres in the air, is a camp gothic roof, which turns out to be an exercise in would-be ecclesiastical post-modern office-block kitsch. And here's an unusual opportunity to gauge your reaction to architectural modernism and post-modernism, because if you haven't been run over crossing the road, you will now be at the end of Leadenhall Street and in a position to appreciate once again how beautiful Richard Rogers' Lloyds Building (1978–86) – a wonderful, spacey group of silver and glass towers – is. As you do so, you overshoot a grubby and undistinguished-looking church on your right. This is St Katherine Cree, one of the survivals of the Great Fire of 1666, and a great example of how not to do it. What could be a lovely, simple early-seventeenth-century interior is ruined by: a) awful plaster portakabin things dominating both side aisles; b) unbelievably kitsch piped (as opposed to pipe) organ music relayed through speakers up and down the church; and c) far too much stained glass.

From here on, City churches largely mean Wren churches built to replace those destroyed in the Great Fire. There are a lot of them, and what follows is one suggestion from among almost any number of routes you could take. Also, many of the churches are pretty well interchangeable – high, light Wren boxes, very beautiful, but often not mutually distinguishable. But you will usually have them much to yourself – a quiet

City Churches

en plein air

City Churches

refuge from the traffic and people outside or a dentist's waiting-room hell of detachment from the real world, depending on how you look at it. I doubt if Wren imagined that his buildings would echo to the unselfconscious opening of coke tins and the munching of sandwiches, but that's about as rowdy as they get nowadays.

Turn right out of St Katherine Cree along Leadenhall Street, then left down Billiter Street and right along Fenchurch Street, pausing to admire the sweet little East End City boys in their pinstripe suits. Then left down Rood Lane, calling in at or passing by St Margaret Pattens Eastcheap, a typical Wren box with a pleasing absence of stained glass and a generally unmucked-about-with interior, some nice old box pews and simple carved choir stalls and organ case. Somebody, bizarrely, seems to have opened a flower shop in the vestibule of the church and then forgotten about it. Carry on to the junction with Tower Street, and look left to the wonderful spire of All Hallows by the Tower. If you're feeling energetic then it's just about worth taking the 200-metre or so stroll down to All Hallows, dating from 675 and with an arch to prove it. Also with a verger who will bounce up to you and tell you more than you really want to know about the place, which is why you need energy to go there. The church was substantially rebuilt in the 1950s following bomb damage, so most of what you see is post-war, including some extremely effectively used concrete (as, for example, the tester, which is quite beautifully moulded). The interior generally is light and pleasing to the eye, largely because of the fine east window. The historic connections – William Penn, Albert Schweitzer, Toc H, ask the verger – make it worth the trip if you like that sort of thing.

Now go back up Tower Street and turn left down St Mary at Hill. Here an undistinguished exterior and an entrance disguised behind a street

City Churches

en plein air

City Churches

doorway and a small courtyard serve as cover for the most stunning, not-to-be-missed interior. This is St Mary at Hill, a remarkable Wren construction which was burnt out in 1988 and rebuilt with commendable sensitivity. A square with interior squares at each corner, separated by barrel vaults, the whole is topped by a fantastic coffered dome. You'll have it to yourself, to get slightly wrong-footed by the surreally beautiful grey decor and equally surreally spaced red conference seats. You'll see what I mean, but only if you try.

Come back out on to St Mary at Hill, turn right down it, and look to your left along St Dunstan's Lane to the Wren tower which is virtually all that remains of St Dunstan's church. Don't bother going to see it close up, but carry on down the road, turn right along Lower Thames Street and cross over to St Magnus the Martyr, another Wren box, this time stacked with (presumably anglo-catholic) camp baroquery.

Back across the road and up King William Street, not bothering to stop at St Clement Eastcheap but instead carrying on to Hawksmoor's St Mary Woolnoth. The best things here are the deeply rusticated exterior, particularly striking in early-morning sunlight, and the astonishing double tower. The interior is formed of a square within a square, the inner one about 1.5 times as high it is broad. There is also some nice old wood, but supermarket muzak destroys the effect.

Go around the corner to St Stephen Walbrook, which is unmissable (and regarded as Wren's smaller masterpiece after St Paul's). The exterior is nothing to write home about, but the interior is superb. It is formed of a rectangle with squared-off corners, the centre surmounted by a fine coffered dome. It was remodelled in the 1980s and now functions on a circular plan echoing the dome, with pews organised in concentric circles around a dramatic circular altar designed by Henry Moore. The inter-

City Churches

en plein air

City Churches

polation of the modern in this interior was a high-risk operation, but the quality is so high it works. And there's real organ music, played by a real organist. I could hardly tear myself away.

Turn left along Queen Victoria Street and engage with the tower of St Mary Aldermary. I can't work out what it is about this tower that makes it so special, but there it is. The interior is worth looking at for the fan vaulting, apparently a Wren pastiche based on the church as it had been before the Great Fire.

Now up Watling Street to St Mary le Bow, of Bow Bells fame. The most exciting thing here is the huge bell-tower, and we can leave it at that.

St Paul's Cathedral (1675–1711). OK, it's a cliché and you didn't want to go there, but you must. After all the other Wren churches, the sheer size of St Paul's is enough to make you feel scared. Walk right around the outside once, and you'll have walked so far you have to go inside to sit down for a rest. When you do so, you will need to take action to avoid being charged ludicrous sums of money or involved in active Christian religious ritual. Possibly the best thing is to go to one of the free organ recitals which take place at reasonably regular intervals. But once you go inside, don't expect to be able to hear any music. For one thing, the visual impact of the nave, the choir, and the dome and transept is such that you'll have enough to cope with anyway. For another thing, the acoustic is simply appalling. I still recollect my first St Paul's concert, sitting under the dome and wondering where all the music had disappeared to. Next time I sat in the nave, and it was worse.

Recover by crossing the road to the improbably named St Vedast-alias-Foster (1670–73). This is a tiny church that very few people visit, so it's quite a relief after St Paul's. Its perfection lies in its simplicity, with banks of pews facing one another across the small rectangular nave.

City Churches

en plein air

City Churches

Now, for the indefatigable, a City churches walk could readily be extended as far again westwards along Fleet Street, or take an alternative route back eastwards. But my guess is that both writers and readers of this guide would rather hop on a bus to the West End, and find a pub to sit down in with a drink and a cigarette. AW

ADDRESS from Christ Church Spitalfields, Commercial Street, London E1 to St Paul's Cathedral, St Paul's Churchyard, London EC4
OPEN most City churches are open weekdays, 9.00–17.00;
St Paul's is open Monday to Saturday, 8.30–16.30, last admission 16.00 (0171-246 8348)
UNDERGROUND Liverpool Street to St Paul's

City Churches

en plein air

Kew Gardens

The approach to Kew Gardens from the station lies along a road which visibly hugs its skirts about it and wishes it were not a public thoroughfare. The Mercedes and BMWs parked outside are pining for high fences and armed guards. Sadly, by charging £5 per head entrance fee, the custodians of the gardens themselves have been made complicit in the miasma of keeping out the riff-raff which hangs over this part of west London. Guiltily, I have to recognise that there is an undeniable spaciousness attendant on the fact that many people can't afford to go to Kew (though the relaxed and uncrowded atmosphere of the place is marred quite badly by the almost claustrophobic impact of the constant noise of aeroplanes coming in to land at Heathrow). I tend to identify three main types of people who come to Kew: Barbour-jacketed parents with wholesome-looking children; rather less wholesome-looking men, trying to find partners for a game of hide-the-sausage as they stroll around the paths and the galleries of the glass-houses; and large groups of sari-clad women having a hilarious time playing at bhaji-on-the-beach. These last seem to have a lot more fun than anybody else, but I don't know how to get invited to join in. So it's more a matter of relishing the frisson of *fin-de-siècle* decay that only a rusting glasshouse can bring.

For those who like such things, the Decimus Burton Temperate House has great big palm trees and things in it, including one billed, Barnum and Bailey style, as the world's largest glasshouse plant. Also impressive is the Palm House (which seems to have things that aren't palms in it), but don't bother with the aquarium underneath – it's full of fish in tanks. Do, however, walk to the eighteenth-century pagoda – the image may be a bit over-familiar, but at ten storeys and c. 50 metres high, the structure is really quite striking. Connoisseurs of the useless should also stop by King William's Temple, an odd, empty neo-classical number built to

Kew Gardens

en plein air

Kew Gardens

commemorate battles fought by the British army between 1760 and 1815. Connoisseurs of food, on the other hand, should probably not try eating at Kew, though for those who can cope with bog-standard municipal-gardens nosh, eating outside in the sun at either the Orangery or the Pavilion restaurants is pretty good.

Perhaps surprisingly, the unmissable thing at Kew is the Princess of Wales conservatory. This is no tacky necrophiliac monument to pink satin, however. Viewed from the right angle, it is a wonderful stack of glass triangles – the greenhouse finds its niche in modernist architecture at last. Inside is a bizarre sculpture garden formed of transcendental cacti and other victims of rampant Darwinism – spiky phalluses and strange lithops buttons.

Speaking of plants, there are quite a lot of them outside. If you conjure up an image of the best-planted municipal park you know, then add a dash of marijuana and a soupçon of the strange, that's what the plant-life at Kew is like. Of course, the creation of a public spectacle is a mere side-show to the main scientific purpose of the gardens. But perhaps it's that sense of being incidental to the main event which produces the heightened awareness that seems part of the place. Either that or some of the exotica have an effect further-reaching than their curators realise. AW

ADDRESS Kew Road, Richmond (0181–332 5000)
OPEN daily, 9.30–16.00, 17.00 or 18.00
ACCESS £5/£2.50 concessions and children 5–16; under-5s free
UNDERGROUND Kew Gardens

Kew Gardens

en plein air

Thames Boat Trip

London has no shortage of pleasures to offer, but there may come times when you feel you've seen enough plays, eaten in enough restaurants, and maybe had one or two more sherries than was quite sensible. In short, what you need is a boat trip.

Real men at this point go out on the Serpentine and make fools of themselves in rowing boats; the rest of us go down to Charing Cross or Westminster piers and find a boat that will take us to the Thames Flood Barrier and back. (There are other trips, but this is the best, though it may involve changing boats at Greenwich.) The tannoyed commentaries on these trips can be a bit irritatingly Jack-the-laddish, but they are also surprisingly informative. In any case, you will have had the sense to make sure that the boat you catch has a bar on it, so what the hell? It's probably best to prime yourself with a tot in advance, because the one time these boats feel a bit quease-making is when they're moving up and down relative to the pontoons at which they moor. Once you're off, however, especially on a fine day, it's absolutely splendid. If you're on the right sort of boat, it should be possible to elbow aside any small children or elderly ladies and get yourself a place on the open deck at the front – or bow, as it is known to us cognoscenti.

It has been said perhaps too often that the Thames is incredibly underused, given that it runs through the middle of London, and incidentally creates a fierce psychological divide as it does so. But it's true: there is very little attention paid to the river, considering how magnificent it is, with some really fine buildings overlooking it. The vantage point you get from the boat is great. The Jack-the-lad will point out to you the National Theatre, Savoy, St Paul's, Globe, Tower of London and goodness knows what else, so I won't try to list them here. The essence of the trip comes later, however, when you've left the attractions of Greenwich behind.

Thames Boat Trip

en plein air

Thames Boat Trip

Down near the slightly disappointing exterior of the Millennium Dome, the river displays that rather scary industrial backside of the city, whose existence you've always suspected, but never before seen quite like this. There is a quay where building aggregates are unloaded on an amazing scale, where the mother and father of all industrial landscapes opens up, with absolutely sculptural conveyor belts, and mysterious processing towers. It is visually stunning, one of those situations in which your awareness of the Other becomes so strong as to make the hairs on the back of your neck prickle. Then on to the flood barrier itself, a string of titanium-clad nodding donkeys ranged across the river, wonderfully dramatic, like a load of miniature Sydney Opera Houses. And on the north bank, just about here, the gigantic scale of this riverine sculpture park is boosted even further by an immense stack of rusty scrap metal. You may think that there's an element of bathos in this description, but believe me, it is visually quite breathtaking.

You won't get the opportunity to disembark at the barrier, so you won't be tempted to visit the barrier visitor centre. That's lucky, because it's quite dreadful – expensive, Stalinist, and infantile. However, I strongly suspect that its sole purpose is to distract the intelligent mind from the realisation that the Thames barrier has absolutely nothing to do with floods, but is simply the most expensive piece of public sculpture in Britain. You'll probably need a large gin and tonic by this stage, and it's just the right thing, as London gradually reasserts its Dr Jekyll side and the boat makes its way back upstream in the late-afternoon sunlight. AW

ADDRESS Victoria Embankment, London SW1 (0891 505471)
ACCESS £7 approximately
UNDERGROUND Embankment/Westminster

Thames Boat Trip

en plein air

cruising

Abney Park Cemetery   6.2
Brompton Cemetery   6.4
Hampstead Heath   6.6

Abney Park Cemetery

> Adieu, farewell earth's bliss.
> This world uncertain is;
> Fond are life's lustful joys
> Death proves them all but toys.
> Thomas Nash (1567–1601), from 'Summers Last Will and Testament'

Abney Park Cemetery is a wonderfully overgrown haven for wild life both human and animal.

'Trees grow from tombs, ivy erases the epitaph from tall pointed obelisks and a forest of flowering shrubs feeds off the dead. In the spring it is a high mass of daffodils, bluebells and cow parsley.

'At times, wraithlike men, some with surprisingly muscular bodies, appear, then disappear in pairs into overgrown abandoned places, no doubt to experience some abandon of their own. Benches on which to meditate and observe are placed strategically along the main paths.'

The above is taken from a letter from a friend, and I find there's little I could add to his description. It's a rare treat indeed to find an open city space that hasn't been overmanicured by the municipal hand. Wandering through the overgrown lanes of memorials, catching a glimpse of the monuments to those who are 'Now asleep', it's possible to forget you're in a city of 8 million people. But as Thomas Nash would remind us: 'Fond are lustful joys, Death proves them all but toys.' And here in the garden of death there is much toying with lustful joy. WM

ADDRESS Stoke Newington Church Street, London N16 (0171-275 7557)
OPEN daily, 8.00–16.00, 17.00, 18.00, 19.00 or 20.00
BUS 73

Abney Park Cemetery

cruising

Brompton Cemetery

Sex and death? I don't think so. Indeed, I rather doubt that the very lively men who pace around Brompton Cemetery on a bright summer's day give much more than a passing thought to the decaying corpses of Victorian dignitaries which lie a few yards beneath their restless feet. *Carpe diem*, innit.

This is the Visconti remake of *The Secret Garden*: vistas of Victorian monumental masonry punctuated by evanescent glimpses of men in shorts and sunglasses. Best of all is the chiaroscuro of the central colonnade, where each slow step holds another pleasing prospect: a Latin type in a turquoise thong sunbathes spead-eagled on an Italianate tomb; a leather jacket swings from the stone curlicue of a shattered crucifix. A Kensington matron walks her dog, oblivious to the possibilities for passion that haunt the air around her.

Actual, rather than potential, passion is somewhat more discreet; people do have regard for the basic decencies, after all (plus a healthy respect for the forces of law and order). But spin off into the shaded shrubberies that line the perimeter walls and you may spot the odd shenanigan. Do go gently. IM

ADDRESS Fulham Road, London SW10 (0171-352 1201)
OPEN daily, 9.00-16.00, 17.00, 18.00 or 19.00
UNDERGROUND Fulham Broadway

cruising

Hampstead Heath

Hampstead Heath has been a recreation ground for Londoners since the eighteenth century. Gone are the wild beasts and highwaymen that once roamed this vast expense of open heath and woodland, to be replaced by a less threatening species of beast who nonetheless demands that you stand and deliver.

Take the path at the end of the carpark behind the Jack Straw's Castle pub at the top of Heath Street and descend carefully to the Heath, where a generous company of expectant fellows may be found. On a moonless night follow the glowing amber of lighted cigarettes dancing like fireflies through the trees, which may lead you to some semblance of your heart's desire.

On a summer's evening, after dusk, the number of men to be found strolling along the paths below the pergola would compete with any nightclub. From time to time various health-education bodies have been known to set up tea trolleys handing out condoms and advice about safer sex. Such public-spirited service is much appreciated, as is the reminder not to leave your rubbish, in any form, behind you. WM

ADDRESS behind Jack Straw's Castle, North End Way, London NW3
OPEN 24 hours
UNDERGROUND Hampstead

Hampstead Heath

cruising

baths/gyms/saunas

Aquarius Sauna	7.2
Chariots Roman Baths	7.6
The Men's Ponds	7.8
The Soho Athletic Club	7.10
YMCA	7.12
York Hall	7.16

Aquarius Sauna

You find this anonymous shop front on Gleneagle Road, painted all blue; there's a number, you ring a bell and they buzz you in. Past the pay desk you find yourself in a small room surrounded by men taking off their clothes. The lockers are miniscule, and after cramming your goods into the smallest of spaces you move through to the next room, a shower area with two doors leading off it. The wooden door reveals a small sauna cabin with room for about ten people; the glass door a tiled steam room with benches. When the steam pours out from beneath the benches, the air becomes opaque, those on the other side of the room lose their features and disappear, and you are left with the two or three men beside you.

It doesn't go any further than that. You come out and take a shower, thinking there must be more. So back you go, through the changing area, up some stairs and you're in a rather large, unkempt house. The floor above has a lounge with TV, where tea, coffee and snacks are on sale. At the bottom of the next staircase is a large trough of condoms and lube. Screened by a partition as you enter, the first room on the next floor has a TV showing videos, with white plastic chairs arranged in a viewing curve. It's up to you whether you watch anything while you're there. The room next door has more partitions with mattresses between, where men spread out, arse up. It might take some time to see them – the lighting is subtle. Even if you don't wear flip flops for the shower area, you might want to put them on for these upper floors.

Up another creaking staircase is the most dilapidated floor. In front of you is a large room with two double beds, and as your eyes grow accustomed to the now-complete darkness you might make out a heap of legs on one of them. I heard groaning coming from one bed and stayed long enough to make out a single large form, rolling around on its own, impossible to say whether in pleasure or loneliness or a mixture of the two. Next

Aquarius Sauna

baths/gyms/saunas

Aquarius Sauna

door to this six or seven partitions create two open sections and a third one farthest from the door which is closed from view. The first and third sections have chairs in them.

There is a mixture here of open and closed spaces, of viewing and obscurity, of committing yourself to complete darkness, nearly naked, and being able, by the way you move or don't, to suggest what you want or don't. It's a little like sex itself. You can get in here and see men of all different sorts and leave again without a word being exchanged. The more control you want, the more will be taken from you. Relax and you can move here like a cipher. Move in and come out unchanged, go back to your normal life. Escape. PJ

ADDRESS 14 Gleneagle Road, London SW16 (0181–769 6998)
OPEN Monday to Thursday, 12.00–24.00; Friday 12.00–Sunday 24.00
MIX men-only
ACCESS £10/£6 before 15.00
BR Streatham (Thameslink from Victoria)

Aquarius Sauna

baths/gyms/saunas

Chariots Roman Baths

In the early 1970s camp British actor and master of *double entendre* Frankie Howerd starred in a sitcom called *Up Pompeii*. Chariots Roman Baths could have been part of the set.

This is one of the largest gay saunas in London, laid out like those of Madrid, Dublin or Amsterdam. There's a large open space, with a good-sized swimming pool in the middle surrounded by daybeds. To one side is a café where friendly staff serve free drinks; there's also a gym with all the usual toning and puffing-up devices to keep you trim and distract you from the other physical pastimes on offer. Amazingly, people have been known to use it. Two corridors of restrooms on the upper floors are well equipped with the accessories to ensure safe but hardly restful pursuits.

Evenings and weekends are busiest, when an assortment of Adonises in all shapes and sizes can be observed wandering from steam room to Jacuzzi to sauna or chilling out in the TV lounge, pre- or post-club. WM

ADDRESS 201–207 Shoreditch High Street, London EC1 (0171-247 5333)
MIX men-only
ACCESS £12
OPEN Monday to Thursday, Sunday, 12.00–24.00; Friday and Saturday, 12.00–9.00
UNDERGROUND Liverpool Street

Chariots Roman Baths

baths/gyms/saunas

The Men's Ponds

The Men's Ponds on Hampstead Heath are one of the few remaining enclaves of male chauvinism. Nude sunbathing is allowed within the screened enclosure, but nude swimming is now prohibited. The ponds are very popular in summer and draw amphibious types of all ages; if you have a weakness for tadpoles and pondweed and would enjoy soaking up the English summer sunshine under the great open skies of the heath, this is the place for you. On the grassy bank outside the entrance can usually be found a number of amicable fellows happy to help you apply the suncream to those places only a wrestler can reach. WM

ADDRESS Hampstead Heath, off Millfield Lane, London N6
OPEN daily; times change seasonally
MIX men-only
ACCESS free
BR Gospel Oak

The Men's Ponds

baths/gyms/saunas

The Soho Athletic Club

The Soho Athletic Club is more than just a gym in that it caters specifically for gay men and women. The giant rainbow flag that spans three storeys of the exterior is a clear statement.

There are the usual instruments of torture to pump you up, keep you trim, or turn you into the sinuous length of muscle that would appear to be the look of the moment. The space is light and airy and the staff are extremely helpful, with personal trainers, both private and employed by the gym, on hand to tailor an exercise package to your needs. The environment is friendly and non-threatening: quiet mid to late morning, busy at lunchtime and after 17.00 and hysterical on Friday evenings and Saturdays when serious preparations for the weekend produce a plethora of Nikidass and sweat.

After your gruelling, or in my case lightly challenging, exercise routine, you can enjoy the excellent sauna facilities or take advantage of the alternative therapies available in the treatment rooms. Advance booking is advised. The café has a good vegetarian menu complemented by a wide assortment of energy-enhancing drinks and a great espresso machine. WM

ADDRESS 10 Macklin Street, London WC2 (0171-242 1290)
OPEN Monday to Friday, 7.00–22.00; Saturday, 10.00–22.00; Sunday, 12.00–18.00
ACCESS day membership £8/£6 before 16.00
UNDERGROUND Covent Garden

The Soho Athletic Club

baths/gyms/saunas

YMCA

On the corner of Great Russell Street and Tottenham Court Road glowers an imposing lump of mid-70s brutalism. The part of the building visible from the street is the YMCA hotel. The gym is below ground level, a vast concrete bunker under central London.

One level down is the pool, looming beautifully out of the concrete. It's lined with dark blue and lit from the sides, and swimming here is a little like swimming at night, as though one had descended into a watery underworld. Members look on from the lounge area through a large wall of glass. Next to this, two levels of concrete balconies are arranged around a giant sports hall with a climbing wall at one end. Weights machines stand in one corner, and along the balconies are cycling, running, rowing and step machines. A separate mirrored room houses free weights.

The arrangement of the gym gives a feeling of great freedom and space, largely thanks to the open central hall, where circuits classes are held throughout the day. And the positioning of the equipment in this open space and around the balconies invites the exerciser to linger and browse. There are great voyeuristic spaces here: two walls of glass looking on to the pool, the main balconies, a viewing gallery around the aerobics room, a glass wall looking on to the dance studio and completely mirrored walls in the two weights rooms. You look down on to the squash court and cardiovascular room, or look up at your audience. There is scarcely anywhere from which it's not possible either to gaze into another space or to see yourself mirrored back.

These open spaces are reflected in the gym's attitude. There is a mix here, and the management made it clear to us that while they welcome their gay members, they don't wish to 'raise the profile of any particular group'. It's an all-inclusive creed. A number of corporate memberships mean that lunchtimes can seem as straight as any other gym, and the excel-

YMCA

baths/gyms/saunas

YMCA

lent exercise classes, from step and aerobics to circuits, attract a large number of women. But come evenings the place has a definitely gay vibe. The club is overwhelmingly friendly: players of badminton, squash or short tennis can add their names and phone numbers to the bottom of a ladder of cards and play their way to the top. Anyone on the board can challenge anyone else. It would be galling indeed if a straight man had thought this one up. There is a strange tension between the lads on the information desk and the camper aerobics instructors. And no one is suggesting they all sing from the same songsheet. But people here do get on. And of course they have a song. PJ

ADDRESS 112 Great Russell Street, London WC1 (0171-637 8131)
OPEN daily, 7.00–22.30
ACCESS various membership prices apply, according to age and whether peak or off-peak; minimum period three months
UNDERGROUND Tottenham Court Road

YMCA

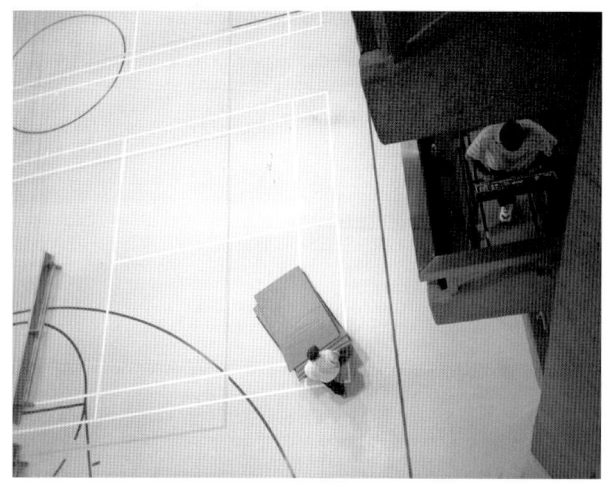

baths/gyms/saunas

York Hall

Perhaps it's the idea of the communal baths of the old East End that casts such a spell – places where men would come to wash together after the day's work. The ground floor of the communal baths at York Hall now houses a vast public swimming pool, a great expanse of blue in which to stretch yourself. In the mid 1980s a dreadlocked Boy George minced around the water's edge here, crooning 'Do You Really Want to Hurt Me?' The real find in this place, however, are the rooms below. Off the main corridor are three tiled areas. Like a Roman baths, these move from tepid, to warm, to sauna-like heat. Men lounge on the wide stone benches, some eyeing you cautiously, others apparently getting away from the family. Outside in the corridor is an icy plunge pool and through another door is the cooler of the two steam rooms. Sit here for long enough and someone will offer you a massage. They lay a towel down on the steaming bench, hose it down with cold water and you gingerly lower yourself on to it. The massage is often very good; afterwards you feel strangely lethargic. A second steam room off the shower area is considerably hotter.

These baths have a large gay clientele and attract men of all sexualities, races, ages and backgrounds. There's an easiness about the place – in the large changing area are loungers for afternoon snoozing – and the facilities are far better than anything you find in the gay saunas. And as the steam rises you can dream up the most unlikely sepia-tinted fantasy. PJ

ADDRESS Old Ford Road, London E2 (0181–980 2243)
OPEN men-only Monday, Tuesday, Thursday and Saturday, 12.00–20.00
ACCESS swim £2.50, steam room £8.50
UNDERGROUND Bethnal Green

York Hall

baths/gyms/saunas

shopping

Expectations	8.2
Gay's the Word	8.4
Prowler Store	8.8
Regulation	8.10
St James's	8.12
Selfridges	8.16

Expectations

Down a steep staircase, the main desk here stands at the centre of a large circular space hung with all kinds of rubber and leather paraphernalia. There are rooms off this main room with racks of leather shirts, piles of porn mags, rubber jockstraps. Curious punters move silently through a techno soundtrack. A large back room has complete suits of rubber, rubber Adidas-style t-shirts and piles of army-surplus gear.

The selection here is similar to Regulation (see page 8.10) – the large rubber dildos, masks, handcuffs – though there is more in the way of fetish trinkets of the cockring, nipple-clamp variety and less of the handcrafted bodybags. Given a little imagination, though, some of the clothing here could be worn by anyone – much of the army surplus stuff is cheap enough and a proportion of the leatherwear is more fashion than fetish.

Expectations caters to a slightly cartoony sexuality. The whole place is painted black, as if to resemble some 1970s view of dungeon life. Although there's a great rubbery-leather smell as you enter, it's mainstream fetish. As society's greatest perverts, we might expect a little more.

PJ

ADDRESS 75 Great Eastern Street, London EC2 (0171–739 0292)
OPEN Monday to Friday, 11.00–19.00; Saturday, 11.00–20.00; Sunday, 12.00–17.00
UNDERGROUND Old Street

Expectations

shopping

Gay's the Word

Marchmont Street is surely an anachronism. It's one of the nicest streets in Bloomsbury, having a sense of community and organic growth about it – and also an organic food shop cum café among a number of small shops, which include Gay's the Word. A definite reminder that the late 1970s/early 1980s weren't all bad.

But at a time when even rather indifferent London bookshops run to a gay and lesbian section, I wonder whether Gay's the Word hasn't begun to miss the point. It attempts a comprehensiveness which is distinctly double-edged – there are whole shelves of (mainly American) books with titles to make your eyes glaze. On the other hand, the selection of academic books on sexuality is quite good, but cannot compete with, say, Dillons or Blackwells. So perhaps this shop falls between two stools. And isn't there a sense of self-absorbed navel-gazing in having on display no fewer than five copies of the engagingly sub-titled *An Oral History of the Gay Liberation Front 1970–1973*? (It's the selection of period which gets me. Also, there's something refreshingly absurd about the proximity of some really quite earnest books to the half dozen copies of *Cocksuck Academy*.) It's amazing to see that 'Coming Out' is still a live enough issue to merit a whole section of shelves devoted to it. I wonder if this may be evidence more of a misguided and anachronistic earnestness than of a real demand (though I am assured this ain't necessarily so). Looking at the men's fiction section convinces me that our desire to identify a literature of our own, while entirely understandable, has generated a terrible over-protectiveness towards the canon. There are some dreadful old warhorses – misogynistic, badly written and plain tedious – which astonishingly are still in print. That's not remotely the fault of Gay's the Word, of course, but it may be a reflection of an almost narcissistic singleness of purpose which has become increasingly hard to justify as times have moved on.

Gay's the Word

shopping

Gay's the Word

I start to wonder whether we, as gay men, are incapable of thinking about anything other than being gay men.

I don't want to push the symbolism too far, but it's the second-hand department which is the real triumph of Gay's the Word. The books are hardly sorted into any kind of order, but that makes the exploration all the more satisfying (and there are only a few hundred of them). There is a terrific range of more or less homosexual twentieth-century literature, including first editions of wonderful gay classics. They are not cheap as second-hand books go, but neither are they overpriced – it's just that an uninhibited burst of enthusiasm could put undue strain on the holiday overdraft.

A pleasant place, then, making up in its sense of community what it may lack in sense of purpose. Events are posted on the noticeboard, and you can pick up a copy of the *Pink Paper*, all of which helps to generate a nice feel of this being a place of our own, where one can relax with the family, so to speak. And pleasant customers, too, gentle herbivores browsing and snuffling their way through the nourishing pages. AW

ADDRESS 66 Marchmont Street, London WC1 (0171–278 7654)
OPEN Monday to Saturday, 10.00–18.30; Sunday, 14.00–18.00
MIX lesbian and gay
UNDERGROUND Russell Square

Gay's the Word

shopping

Prowler Store

Located on the corner of Brewer and Rupert Streets, Prowler is an emporium of all things dolly. Whereas the other gay sex shops are very black, Prowler is bright, glowing white; whereas the soundtrack elsewhere is techno, here it's handbag and showtunes. The shop has its range of sex toys and fetish paraphernalia, but it gives over most of its space to clothing, watches, greetings cards, books, CDs, videos and endless reproductions of the rainbow flag. A mixture of camp lifestyle and beefy pin-ups, this is more a gift shop than a sex shop, a kind of vanilla fudge. PJ

ADDRESS 3–7 Brewer Street, London W1 (0171-734 4031)
OPEN Monday to Thursday, 11.00–21.00; Friday and Saturday, 11.00–24.00; Sunday, 10.00–20.00
UNDERGROUND Piccadilly Circus

Prowler Store

shopping

Regulation

8.10

The first thing you notice when they buzz you into this large warehouse-type shop off Islington Green is the overwhelming smell of rubber and leather. It boasts more than 2000 lines, apparently endless racks of leather, rubber and militaria, everything the committed fetishist needs: fireman uniforms, frogman outfits, sailor suits, every kind of vintage army and naval uniform. In the second bay a man is struggling with a pile of gasmasks – a faint whiff of war poetry – and like some apocalyptic Virgin Mary a mannequin looms in a black rubber suit with rubber veil and mask. There are hoses spewing out of wooden crates, waders up to here and, along the tops of the racks, pair upon pair of gumboots. There are jocks, harnesses, facemasks, pumps, a whole rack of handcuffs, some nappies and, haphazard on a low table, a pile of huge black cellophane-wrapped dildos, lying like discarded rubber limbs.

The man I talk to at the counter indicates a large workshop to the side where garments can be altered or articles made to customers' requirements. The shop will repair all gear bought there and makes goods for the US, Japan, Europe – it's not just us, you know. He gives me a catalogue and at home I peruse the things I have missed: the straitjacket, the (inflatable) bodybag, the (inflatable) blindfold, the drainage bag, vacuum bags, the master-slave respirator, the abattoir apron, the rubber gloves … as though all that we do were just this pumping up and letting down. PJ

ADDRESS 17A St Alban's Place, London N1 (0171–226 0665)
OPEN Monday to Saturday, 10.30–18.30; Sunday, 12.00–17.00
UNDERGROUND Angel

Regulation

shopping

St James's

Readers of P G Wodehouse will be familiar with the ethos of St James's. Even today, although their younger counterparts have mainly departed for Notting Hill and Hell-on-Chelsea Harbour, gents of a certain age and uncertain orientation can still be seen plying their age-old profession of strolling, perfectly attired, in pursuit of the perfect shirt, prior to taking a leisurely lunch in some ghastly club. While some submission to postwar vulgarity is visible along Jermyn Street, there is still a palpable style to many of the shops. Shirt-makers are a dime a dozen around here, and it's not worth singling out any for special mention, because all their shop-window displays are frankly gorgeous. Only the outrageousness of their names serves to establish a pecking order.

It's probably easiest to start by going through to Jermyn Street from Piccadilly, down the alley which runs along the side of St James's Church (see page 11.26). Then turn right and look at some of the shops. Apart from having a pleasingly old-fashioned manner, Paxton and Whitfield is probably the second-best cheese shop in London, conducted without the innovative approach of Neal's Yard, but with considerably more panache. Next stop is Floris, the perfumiers. Floris rose geranium soap had a quaint role in immortalising Syrie Maugham, in that she provided it for guests at her house in the south of France, and this fact was cited by Beverley Nichols as proving what a good soul she was and how betrayed by Somerset. That seems to justify the term 'legendary' for that particular product (now, I believe, discontinued because of its failure to find a sufficient market in the Americas). Floris still has a wonderful air to it, and some of the most lovely bath and shave additives in the world.

Resist, for the moment, popping into Fortnum's for tea, and instead carry on down Jermyn Street buying as many shirts as you can afford. At St James's Street pause to revel in the glorious vulgarity of Davidoff's

St James's

shopping

St James's

cigar shop on the corner, and then turn left. First note the window display in Lobb, possibly the most upmarket shoe-makers in the world. Three pairs of uninspiring-looking black shoes and a pair of cowboy boots seems to go beyond any snooty 'We don't need to advertise' and to become a subtle test which potential customers must pass. Perhaps I'll stick to Clarks. Almost next door is Lock's the hatter. Again there is something rather off-putting about the window display, but it does at least contain hats which you might want to wear. In fact, Lock's is a super shop; the products are great and the service comfortable and stylish.

On now to Berry Brothers and Rudd, where they have been selling wine since the seventeenth century (possibly in the same shop). Here, the low, black entrance gives on to a room with bare floorboards and comfortable old furniture. You sit and look at the list, and in due course decide what you want to order. A pinstriped gent will then go down to the cellar to fetch your dozen Pichon-Lalande '78 – or in my case, a couple of bottles of their 'good ordinary claret' for the same price as the equivalent in a supermarket. Worth noting also that Berry Bros sells the best wine glasses in the world, handmade English crystal, and they are not expensive for what they are.

Finally back along King Street, past all the fine-art auction houses, and into St James's Square, noting the extreme ordinariness of the façade of the London Library in passing. And so back up to Jermyn Street, and to Fortnum's for tea. AW

ADDRESS start at Piccadilly, London W1
UNDERGROUND Piccadilly Circus

St James's

shopping

Selfridges

Thankfully the dimmest of the European/American rich kids who are such a drawback to shopping will be at the nightmare on Knightsbridge. But there are still enough of them in Selfridges. Given its location near where the downmarket tackiness of Oxford Street meets the upmarket tackiness of Bond Street, you would expect the prime distinguishing feature of Selfridges to be, er, tackiness. In fact the store is undergoing a species of post-modern angst, which is resolved in quite a stylish manner.

There is a tension between the undeniable grandeur of the exterior (clock especially the clock) and the disconnectedness of much of the interior. There is something of the upmarket souk about the store, though it possesses a stylishness totally unknown in middle-eastern street markets. Quaint pockets of old-fashioned respectability are retained here and there, and it is possible to detect traces of the establishment in which Paddington Bear disgraced himself. The management's efforts to refashion the store so as to attract the Prada junkies has been resisted by the shop's own attachment to the hideous suburban tat which was the hallmark of department stores across the land from the late nineteenth century until they all went bankrupt in 1983. The result in this case is a pleasing ambiguity, in which you move easily from an active interest in buying in some departments to an appalled fascination in others.

The good. The men's clothes department probably has as eclectic a range of stuff as you will find anywhere – Hilfiger through Kenzo to Chester Barrie – and prices are comparatively reasonable. Now find your way to the back of the ground floor, to the food hall. The fish counter alone serves to expose as lazy tosh the stuff which still pollutes the Sunday press about how all Brits eat overcooked cabbage and burned meat, while everything in France is wonderful. Then to the cookery department in the basement. I think it must be the le cruisey effect that guarantees that there

Selfridges

shopping

Selfridges

are more queens to the square yard in cookery departments up and down the country than in any comparable spaces other than lorry-parks.

The bad. The basement book department must be the place in which they compile the best-seller lists which show the English vainly trying to prove they aren't illiterate. It's just possible to distinguish the fake books on sale from the fake books with which somebody has decorated the department. In a fit of so-called post-modern irony? I don't think so.

And the necessary. There are about a dozen places for eating and drinking in Selfridges. Personally, I prefer to lunch sparingly off a glass of wine and a cigarette, for which purpose the first-floor winebar/café is fine. (It also has quite good snacks, sandwiches and salads.) For those who feel the need of something a little more substantial, there is a quite serious restaurant on the third floor. Otherwise, the possibilities range from the expensive but good Oyster Bar on the ground floor through a range of OK places to an awful coffeeshop affair which looks to have been transported direct from the Guildford branch of Debenhams. Here, prosperous unemployed women wearing scarves exchange malicious gossip and look forward to the end of another trying day. Meanwhile, I, the gay anti-shopper, come away after spending hours in the place and enjoying it. They must be doing something right. AW

ADDRESS 400 Oxford Street, London W1 (0171-629 1234)
OPEN Monday to Wednesday, 10.00–19.00; Thursday and Friday, 10.00–20.00; Saturday, 9.30–19.00; Sunday, 12.00–18.00
UNDERGROUND Bond Street

Selfridges

shopping

markets

Brick Lane 9.2
Camden Lock Market 9.6
Columbia Road Flower Market 9.8

Brick Lane

This traditionally poor neighbourhood between the City and the river has provided a sanctuary for newly arrived immigrants for hundreds of years. In the seventeenth and eighteenth centuries the Huguenots, fleeing religious persecution in continental Europe, established a flourishing silk-weaving industry. In the nineteenth century Jews, many originally on their way to the United States from the oppressive regime of the Russian empire, settled in the area and turned their skills to the rag trade, which still flourishes.

But the latest group to take up residence in this part of London's East End are the Bengalis, who have yet again reinvented the neighbourhood. The large building on the corner of Brick Lane and Fournier Street has in its time been a French church, a Methodist chapel and a synagogue, and is now a mosque.

Brick Lane is also participating in the transformation that is overtaking the City fringes – like Shoreditch and Clerkenwell, artists and designers are moving in. The most noticeable change is the development of the enormous Truman's Brewery site, now home to clubs, bars, shops and exhibition spaces, locations for a thousand fashion shoots and music videos.

On Sunday the whole area becomes a bustling market, beginning at the junction of Brick Lane and Bethnal Green Road and stretching up to Shoreditch High Street. The busiest section spills out along Cheshire Street and Sclater Street. Here you can find everything from carburettors to 1950s glassware, furniture to CDs, much of which never even made it on to the back of the lorry. Beware: videos are often a bad buy, pirated and of poor quality.

Beigel Bake at 159 Brick Lane is worth a visit. Much frequented by marketers, taxi drivers and clubbers on their way home, it's open 24 hours and sells every type of bagel and filling imaginable.

Brick Lane

markets

Brick Lane

But Brick Lane really comes into its own on weekday evenings. Just after dusk the brilliant colours of the sari shops dazzle and the latest Bangra and Hindi tunes assault the ears. Men and boys dressed in white with beautifully embroidered skull caps stand around the entrance to the mosque laughing and chatting as you head off for what has been described as the best Indian food in London.

The most popular restaurants are the Clifton at 126 and the Nazrul at 130 (but see below). Here you will be served dish after dish of exquisite food at a price it's hard to believe.

On 17, 24 and 30 April bombs were planted in Brixton, the Brick Lane area and Soho, aimed at causing fear and death within the Afro-Caribbean, Bengali and gay communities. Fortunately, thanks to the quick thinking of a Brick Lane resident who found the bomb and placed it in the boot of his car to take it to the local police station, carnage in these narrow, busy streets was avoided. The bomb did explode, wrecking several local businesses including the Nazrul restaurant, but no one in this instance was severely hurt. While Tony Blair may applaud the contribution made by ethnic and sexual minorities to Cool Britannia, these acts of senseless violence are a reminder that there are members of society who – due to ignorance, bigotry, deep-rooted racism or unadulterated hatred – would prefer us to go back to somewhere that for many no longer exists, in our case the closet. Well forget it, we're here to stay. WM

ADDRESS Brick Lane, London E2
OPEN market open Sundays, 8.00–13.00
UNDERGROUND Aldgate East

Brick Lane

markets

Camden Lock Market

Camden Town is no longer the Irish ghetto it was in the 1950s, though relics of its past, such as the Gay Celidgh held every second month at the Camden Irish Centre in Murray Street, remain.

Camden Lock Market is a space where hippies, rockabillies, punks, new romantics and goths live on amid a sprinkling of new-age crystal culture. The section nearest to Camden Town Underground is dedicated to the prevailing narcissism of the moment; plough through that and you arrive at the canal lock, passing Zipper Store – which stocks the usual array of exotic toys for boys, magazines and videos – at 283 Camden High Street on your way.

At the side of the lock is the Dingwall Gallery, spread over three floors and housing a haphazard collection of stalls selling crafts, artworks, jewellery and completely useless ornaments of varying design and quality. In the stable yard is the second-hand section: furniture, books, clothes and antiques laid out in a maze of arches and old stables where the horses that pulled the barges along the Regent's Canal once rested. Food is readily available from the stalls near the canal and the aroma of Thai noodles, coffee and baked potatoes fills the air. The market is busiest on Saturdays and Sundays – go early if you want to avoid the coachloads of tourists. WM

ADDRESS Camden Lock Place, London NW1
OPEN market open daily, 9.30–17.00
UNDERGROUND Camden Town

Camden Lock Market

markets

Columbia Road Flower Market

Flower Market. 5.4.98.
You: red polo neck, from Clerkenwell. Me: black donkey jacket, met in the crush by the palm stall. Yes, it does look great, but I need those gardening tips and to feel the warmth of your smile again. Do get in touch. Peter. Box V156 R.

Columbia Road Flower Market is very much part of the London gay experience. Whether you've just fallen out of a club or all-night sauna and need that chill-out factor, or have woken rejoicing at the lack of a hangover with a stubbled chin and soft pair of lips brushing your ear to whisper 'breakfast', then Columbia Road is the place to go.

The street is typical of London's East End: two-storey terraced houses with shops on the ground floor and a pub at each end. The market has been established for more than ten years and the shops sell a variety of goods from second-hand furniture to hats. The old workshops to the back and side of the market have been taken over by potters, furniture-makers, craft-sellers and interior decorators. There are also stalls selling jewellery, and more cafés than you could possibly need. But the main business of the morning is flowers and plants.

The traders set up at 7.00. An hour later all you can see is a blaze of colour from one end of the market to the other. Shouts of 'Get your nigella damascena, six for a fiver' and 'Amaranthus caudatus, 50 pence each' ring through the air – and depending on the success of your Saturday night, 'love-in-a-mist' or 'love-lies-bleeding' may be just how you feel. By 11.00 the market is very busy and genial crushes form in the narrow thoroughfare between the stalls. There's nothing that quite matches the frisson of eye contact through exotic stems of birds of paradise followed by the realisation that the owner of those lavender eyes is

Columbia Road Flower Market

markets

Columbia Road Flower Market

sitting opposite you at Jones' Dairy in Ezra Street, grinning over the brim of a mug of coffee.

The courtyard in Ezra Street, just off the market down the side of the Royal Oak pub (see page 2.14 – gay newspapers and cooked breakfasts available in the upstairs room) is a warren of shops and studios. Look out for Stoney Parson's stained-glass workshop where Stoney and her partner Rachel make glass panels and other smaller, inexpensive objects. Just around the corner is Jones' Dairy and café for delicious smoked salmon and cream-cheese bagels, pastries and cakes washed down with good fresh coffee or tea. The clientele is mixed, but I'd guarantee there'll be more than enough distractions to take your mind off your herbaceous border. WM

ADDRESS Columbia Road, London E2
OPEN Sundays, 8.00–13.00
BUS 8, 26, 55, 67, 149

Columbia Road Flower Market

markets

museums and galleries

British Library 10.2
Leighton House 10.6
Museum of London 10.10
National Portrait Gallery 10.14
Sir John Soane's Museum 10.22

British Library

You need a reader's pass to get the full experience of the British Library, and they are not particularly easy to come by. But even without a pass, the new building is well worth a visit. Don't be put off by the rather bleak open space in front, nor by the austerity of the brick façade. There is a pre-Thatcherite sense of solidity and worth about the architecture – lavatories, restaurants, even the telephone booths are all done to a specification hardly ever (never?) seen in modern public buildings in Britain.

The core of the complex is the c. 25-metre-high glass tower which houses the King George IV collection of books, displayed with their spines facing outwards through the glass, to odd, slightly subversive effect. To the left of this, the Ritblat Gallery has on display examples of early illumination, printing and binding: it all feels a bit overwhelming to the non-specialist, but there's still something impressive about finding yourself face to face with Magna Carta or the Gutenberg or Caxton Bibles.

Lunch in the first-floor restaurant features reasonablish food (but avoid the ludicrously expensive wine), well-designed cutlery, a pleasant space, and one of the best people-watching opportunities in London. Of course, a high percentage of Library regulars are pompous or hideously eccentric, but there is also a much greater than average proportion of the truly eminent and the positively angelic-looking. Anyway, they all have to have lunch somewhere, and a fair number can be seen in the restaurant.

For those with reader's passes, there is a choice of reading rooms in which to work. The striking main Humanities room feels like a well-designed ant hill, with stakhanovite intellectual slaves and cultured dilettantes working side by side. There is a pleasing matiness among the readers, probably the product of a shared routine and mystique. The interior rises perhaps 20 metres to the white-metal and glass ceiling, while at ground level the high-quality modern leather and wood desks and

British Library

museums and galleries

British Library

chairs provide a solid base from which to read, write, or wonder whether the man at the opposite desk might be available.

Up two floors, the Cotton Room – a kind of recreation space for readers – is almost a return to the underfunded-polytechnic ambience the rest of the library so successfully avoids. But the outside terrace is wonderful, with a terrific view over King's Cross and St Pancras stations, the spectacular ironwork of the gas holders off Pancras Road, and points north.

Have tea in the ground-floor café, which sells very good cake and rather expensive cups of tea, served – if you choose the right moment – by some of the campest counter staff in Western Europe. Most customers, particularly as the light fades in the late afternoon in winter, can be seen looking nervously at the eerily unlit centre tables, wondering how one could satisfactorily resolve the lighting problem posed by the fact that the ceiling at this point must be about 25 metres high. Architect Colin St John Wilson evidently gave up on that one.

For all the fuss about cost overruns and unadventurous functionality, the actual experience of this building is that it not only works, but is sufficiently enjoyable in its own right to be worth including in the London itinerary. AW

ADDRESS Euston Road, London NW1 (0171-412 7676)
OPEN Monday and Thursday, 9.30–18.00; Tuesday and Wednesday, 9.30–20.00; Friday and Saturday 9.30–17.00
ACCESS exhibition spaces, bookshop, restaurant and café open to public; collections open to ticket-holders only
UNDERGROUND Euston, King's Cross

British Library

museums and galleries

Leighton House

Lord Frederic Leighton (1830–1896), painter and admirer of handsome young men, lived here for 30 years. He commissioned architect and fellow Royal Academician George Aitchison to build the house and studio in 1864.

The severe Victorian brick façade masks the splendour that lies within – a contradiction that could be seen as symbolic of Leighton the man and of the time in which he lived. Though it was widely known within the art world that Leighton was a homosexual, it could have proved disastrous had this become public knowledge – as was the case with Oscar Wilde. Many believe that Leighton's inability to express himself freely had a detrimental influence on his painting, but such bronzes as *Athlete Struggling with a Python* and *The Sluggard* reveal his inner sensuality. And whoever enters the portals of Leighton House will discover an aesthete's palace.

The Arab Hall (featured in the film *The Wings of the Dove*) is the centrepiece of this decorator's paradise. Two pillars frame the entrance to a Moorish internal courtyard. In the middle is a sunken black marble pool, whose clear water reflects the gilt mosaic frieze, decorative blue wall tiles and gold dome above. The tiles date mostly from the sixteenth and seventeenth centuries and were collected from all over the Islamic world. Looking on to the courtyard from above are the finely carved panels of the Zenana that Leighton brought back from Cairo. This is the world of the Arabian Nights.

The main feature of the drawing room is the chimneypiece, which surprisingly is situated beneath a window. The flue rises to the left and a glass shutter slides over from the right. Aitchison designed this feature to give an optical illusion of endless rooms when seen from the library across the hall.

Leighton House

museums and galleries

Leighton House

The staircase curves around past the Silk Room and leads into a studio of magnificent proportions where Leighton painted his models, usually guardsmen, while 'sacrificing himself to the muses'. WM

ADDRESS 12 Holland Park Road, London W14 (0171-602 3316)
OPEN Monday to Saturday, 11.00–17.00
ACCESS free
UNDERGROUND Kensington High Street

Leighton House

museums and galleries

Museum of London

This compact, cleverly designed museum is hidden in the heart of the City in an area that has been inhabited since prehistoric times. The 12 galleries are laid out in chronological order around a central garden that charts the history of nursery gardens from the Saxon period to the present.

The Roman gallery looks out on to part of the London wall and a semi-ruined tower of one of the city's former gates. There are wall paintings from a Roman bath house found beneath the ruins of the medieval Winchester Palace in Southwark and mosaics discovered during the 1860s which indicate how elaborate Roman houses must have been. Olive oil and wine are not only fads of the 1990s – to judge by the amount of pots and jars found by the Thames, this northern outpost of the empire hankered after Mediterranean tastes even then. The mysterious cult of Mithras was apparently popular among legionnaires – a men-only affair like many clubs today. With the withdrawal of the legions, however, the city was slowly abandoned, only to be re-established some 200 years later. The Dark Ages had begun.

Subsequent galleries take us from the Saxon invasions through the unification of the English kingdoms in the medieval era to the flowering of a nation state under the Tudors. It's during the Stuart period that the London we know today began to take shape, as the theatres and brothels on the south bank of the river and the timbered lanes and alleys were swept away by the Great Fire of 1666 to be replaced by familiar landmarks including Wren's St Paul's Cathedral and the many steeples of the London skyline (see pages 5.6–5.16). The achievements of the eighteenth and nineteenth centuries are easily recognisable to us – these are the streets and bridges we walk along and the houses and flats we live in.

The London Now section of the museum reflects the ever-changing

Museum of London

museums and galleries

Museum of London

face of the city from the arrival of immigrants from the Caribbean on the HMS *Windrush* in the 1950s. The Catwalk – bright green in colour – provides a fast-track route through the museum and contains computers with interactive displays in five languages.

Lunch in the museum café is recommended. WM

ADDRESS London Wall, London EC2 (0171–600 3699/0807)
OPEN Monday to Saturday, 10.00–17.50; Sunday, 12.00–17.50
ACCESS £5/£3 children and concessions
UNDERGROUND St Paul's/Barbican

museums and galleries

National Portrait Gallery

The National Portrait Gallery is perhaps the nation's greatest monument to the contributions made by gay men and women to the worlds of politics, the arts and science.

Enter the gallery from St Martin's Place and take the staircase or lift to the third floor. Alongside the portrait of Sir Thomas More and his family is that of his friend, the great Dutch humanist Desiderius Erasmus (1469–1536). In the years preceding the Reformation Erasmus became famous throughout Europe for his sermons on pacifism and tolerance. The Pope eventually granted him a dispensation from his monastic vows after wrangling with his abbot Servatious, with whom Erasmus had been in love in his youth.

In Room 24 is a portrait of Lord Frederic Leighton (see page 10.6) by Thomas Brock. On either side of the doorway are portraits of Charles Ricketts (1866–1931) and Charles Shannon (1863–1937), painted by Shannon. The pair met while they were studying at the City and Guilds Technical Art School in Lambeth and spent the next 50 years together. Ricketts became a fine illustrator and Shannon a successful portrait painter and lithographer. They established the Vale Press in 1899, which published most of Oscar Wilde's work in illustrated editions. In 1915 Ricketts was offered the directorship of the National Gallery, but he turned it down when his requests to have the walls covered in watered silk and flowers placed in all the rooms were refused. While hanging paintings in his studio Shannon fell from a ladder and as a result remained a physical and mental invalid for the rest of his life. No longer able to communicate with his partner, Ricketts was inconsolable and died two years later.

Room 19 has a striking portrait of Earl Kitchener of Khartoum (1850–1916) – best known for the relief of Khartoum after the murder of General

National Portrait Gallery

museums and galleries

National Portrait Gallery

Gordon (1885) and for the defeat of the Khalifa at Omdurman (1898) – painted by Sir Herbert Von Herkomer. Kitchener's face became a symbol of patriotism during World War 1 when he appeared on a recruitment poster, index finger pointing outwards, with the slogan, 'Your country needs YOU.' Kitchener handpicked the handsome, unmarried young officers who served under him. They became known as 'Kitchener's band of boys' and were fiercely loyal to their leader. In 1904 he met Captain Oswald Fitzgerald of the 18th Bengal Lancers. A mutual friend observed that, 'Never was there a stronger or more loyal bond than that which these two men had for one another.' That the two lived together openly caused a certain amount of comment, as did Kitchener's passion for flower arranging and collecting porcelain. They died together when their ship HMS *Hampshire* struck a mine off the Orkney coast. Fitzgerald's body was washed ashore but Kitchener was never seen again.

In room 26 is a beautiful sculpture of T E Lawrence ('Lawrence of Arabia', 1888–1935) by E H Kennington. Beside his head are represented the three books he carried throughout the Arab Revolt (1917–18): *The Oxford Book of English Verse*, the *Morte d'Arthur* and a Greek anthology. His own book, *The Seven Pillars of Wisdom*, is dedicated to S.A. – Salem Ahmed, who was 14 years old when Lawrence first met him while working on an archaeological dig in Syria before the war. *The Seven Pillars* opens with a cryptic poem which hints that it was for SA's sake that Lawrence fought and suffered for the cause of Arab independence: 'I loved you, so I drew these tides of men into my hands and wrote my will across the sky in stars to gain you Freedom ...'

John Gunston's photograph of war poet Wilfred Owen (1893–1918) captures a youth in officer's uniform who was to be sacrificed in a pointless war. At one point an exploding shell blew Owen into a trench, where

National Portrait Gallery

museums and galleries

National Portrait Gallery

he spent several days trapped by the firing with only the dismembered body of a fellow officer for company. He ended up at Craiglockhart war hospital near Edinburgh where he met Siegfried Sassoon, who provided him with the emotional and literary catalysts that enabled him to produce such poems as 'Anthem for a Doomed Youth'. Owen was killed in action just seven days before the war ended.

Room 27, designed by Piers Gough, is a celebration of the gay contribution to the early twentieth century. A pastel by Simon Bussy depicts Lytton Strachey (1880–1932), a biographer famous for his dictum: 'Discretion is not the better part of biography.' A member of the Bloomsbury Group of writers and artists, Strachey is best known for his work *Eminent Victorians* and for his relationship with artist Dora Carrington, who tolerated his many boyfriends and his promiscuity. As a conscientious objector during World War 1, Strachey was asked by a recruitment officer what he would do if a German soldier tried to rape his sister. His reply: 'I should attempt to interpose my body.'

English post-impressionist Duncan Grant, Strachey's cousin and lover, is here too, as is economist John Maynard Keynes, who had affairs with both Strachey and Grant. There is a haunting self-portrait by Denton Welch, while novelist E M Forster, looking rather like a 1930s bank manager, hides a well of sensuality behind a respectable façade. Benjamin Britten and Peter Pears sit side by side, united by their love of each other and of music. And the sophisticate Noël Coward gives us all one of his languid smiles.

The ground floor of the gallery is dedicated to late-twentieth-century icons. The bronze of Francis Bacon by Clive Barker is frighteningly realistic. The cold New York winter is the setting for Richard Avedon's 1966 photograph of W H Auden, poet in exile. David Thompson's moving

National Portrait Gallery

museums and galleries

National Portrait Gallery

portrait of film-maker and gay activist Derek Jarman reminds us of yet another great artist and brave man lost to the scourge of AIDS. The actor Sir Dirk Bogarde, star of *Victim*, *The Servant* and *Death in Venice*, looks on wistfully from a painting by David Tindle. Andy Warhol's portrait of Joan Collins is a tribute to hairdressers the world over, and there is a wonderful photograph of the venerable thespian Sir John Gielgud jumping for joy and grinning wickedly. David Hockney is doubly represented by a self-portrait and a painting of novelist Christopher Isherwood and his lover Don Bachardy. And don't miss the provocatively voyeuristic print of dancer Michael Clark by David Buckland.

In a small side gallery is a photograph of John Wolfenden (1906–1985), responsible for the Wolfenden Report on Homosexual Offences and Prostitution that resulted in the 1967 Sexual Offences Act which decriminalised certain homosexual acts. Wolfenden's brilliant son Jeremy, a journalist and secret agent, was openly gay and died tragically, allegedly of alcohol abuse, in New York in 1965.

One of the gallery's latest acquisitions is a portrait of Chris Smith, the openly gay Secretary of State for Culture, Media and Sport. Though the New Labour government has a more positive attitude towards gay people than its predecessor in power, our contribution to society and to the world at large is rarely given the recognition it deserves. But where would the National Portrait Gallery be without us? WM

ADDRESS St Martin's Place, London WC2 (0171-306 0055)
OPEN Monday to Saturday, 10.00–18.00; Sunday, 12.00–18.00
ACCESS permanent collection, free
UNDERGROUND Trafalgar Square

National Portrait Gallery

museums and galleries

Sir John Soane's Museum

Do not go to the Soane Museum drunk or stoned. It is such a disorienting place that to gild the lily is to risk madness. The term *trompe l'oeil* may well have been coined especially for this museum. Few things are quite what they seem. Every way through from room to room turns out to be a mirror, except for the mirror over there, which is actually an internal window on to another room, and you can't find your way round to it, and it's a bit like a bad dream until finally you realise that the fat man over there looking at a case of antique coins is blocking the only way through, which in any case is disguised as a statue. I'm not exaggerating.

Bank of England architect Sir John Soane (1753–1837) bought three neighbouring houses on the north side of Lincoln's Inn Fields to house himself, his family, and his collection of books, paintings and antique knick-knacks. Then he turned his considerable intelligence, imagination and energy to the task of making it weird. Part of the subversive effect lies in the fact that this is in some ways a simulacrum of an early-nineteenth-century family home, in which mamma and papa brought up their dear children to believe in god, the family and the British empire. But Sir John Soane was a lousy father, and it may be that some of the hatred and paranoia which suffused his family life have rubbed off on the fabric of these strange buildings.

The administration of the place is incomparably good. You ring the front doorbell, to be admitted by slightly fierce but harmless staff. Thereafter, knowledgeable but eccentric people will tell you incomprehensibly obscure facts about the museum's contents, or leave you alone, if that's what you prefer. You must, however, let the staff demonstrate the picture room. Soane decided to maximise the space here by building hinged fake walls, layered one on the other, thereby getting six times more hanging space. And the effect is really remarkable, especially when the peculiar

Sir John Soane's Museum

museums and galleries

Sir John Soane's Museum

man demonstrating how it all works shines inadequate torch light on some obscure engraving, and goes into minute detail about it, but forgets to mention that the Hogarth *Rake's Progress* is the original.

Another problem is that one is so shocked by the strangeness of the layout and design that one forgets to look at the contents properly. And though some of the Greek and Roman stuff is of pretty dubious provenance, there is a fair quantity that is good – if you can make it out in the prevailing gloom. The lighting levels which are affected here are probably genuine eighteenth century.

The basement sculpture rooms are good for hide and seek, but again, be careful to hold on to your sanity. Much of the display area was built as sort of outhousing by Soane, and it is extremely difficult to work out whether you're inside or outside the main house, and how to get from one room to another.

Back to the living quarters, where the strength of the colours is enough to give you a bit of a headache, made worse by the fact that nearly everything is doing its damnedest to be something else – wood is painted like marble, marble like wood, false ceilings abound.

Emerge dying for a cup of tea – and hard cheese. There's no room for a café in the museum, and not very much available nearby, apart from the rather scruffy outdoor affair in the middle of Lincoln's Inn Fields, which you will have to share with lawyers and other alcoholic low-life. AW

ADDRESS 13 Lincolns Inn Fields, London WC2 (0171-405 2107)
OPEN Tuesday to Saturday, 10.00–17.00; first Tuesday of the month 18.00–21.00
ACCESS free
UNDERGROUND Holborn

Sir John Soane's Museum

museums and galleries

theatres and concerts

Conway Hall 11.2
Drill Hall 11.6
Glyndebourne 11.10
Holland Park Music and Dance Festival 11.14
Kenwood Music Festival 11.16
Lyric Theatre 11.20
Music in Churches 11.24

Conway Hall

How odd to suggest visiting this scruffy, undistinguished place – the very essence of worthiness and do-goodery. The Conway Hall was indeed the site of some stormy and celebratory gay-rights meetings in the 1970s and 1980s, but that's not why you should go there – it's the music. South Place Sunday Concerts have been taking place on Sunday evenings in winter for well over 100 years, and they have been in the Conway Hall since it was built in 1929. And it is extraordinary. The most famous string-quartet players in the world – people like the old Amadeus or Lindsay quartets – include in their global tour schedule a one-off in this slightly dusty, shabby venue, with its slightly dusty, shabby audience.

Of course, this is a little unfair. Until quite recently it was the case that the audience was composed largely of personal friends and approximate contemporaries of the late George Bernard Shaw. Mild socialist humanism was much in evidence, together with white hair, deaf aids, sandals and some of the most outrageous absence of couture awareness to be seen anywhere. As these gathered, preparations for the performance would be made: an elderly goblin wearing a pullover with several enormous holes in it would arrange chairs for the players around a standard lamp *circa* 1943, with a fringed lampshade. And, in due course, the Amadeus String Quartet would appear and deliver a performance of Beethoven and Shostakovich for which New Yorkers would have killed to get tickets.

Sadly, neither the goblin nor the Amadeus Quartet is still with us. But the standard lamp lives on, as do the stunning performances. The audience is now very much more mixed than it used to be, with a discernible gay element – not yet in its dotage. And though some members may look a bit peculiar, you will rarely find a more musically knowledgeable group of people gathered in one spot – nor yet a more friendly and

Conway Hall

theatres and concerts

Conway Hall

outgoing one. Be a little careful, though: if you sit in the wrong place you will be told about it (especially in the 'season ticket holders only' seats in the gallery).

Why go, then, to this obscure hall with its bare boards and undistinguished decor, its forbidding conventions surrounding the very ordinary tea and coffee to be drunk at the interval, with no bar, far less a café or restaurant? First, it's amazingly cheap. Then the range and quality of the programming – a typical season will embrace top-class performances of some of the finest chamber-music repertoire, together with some unfamiliar new works. And this is the space in which to hear chamber music, probably the best acoustic for the purpose in London, and to my mind noticeably superior to the Wigmore Hall. Then there are the people – and even on a first visit you are likely to find yourself in conversation with somebody whose life turns out to be extraordinary.

Unfortunately, many of the local pubs close on Sundays – a particular shame in the case of the Princess Louise, since Sunday used to be the one day when it was sufficiently uncrowded to appreciate its magnificent interior, and the splendid men's lavatory. So interval and post-concert drinks are taken in the agreeable Dolphin along the street. AW

ADDRESS 25 Red Lion Square, London WC1 (0171-242 8032)
OPEN Sundays, 18.00 for 18.30
ACCESS £4/under-16s free
UNDERGROUND Holborn

Conway Hall

theatres and concerts

Drill Hall

It's hard to avoid being unfair to the Drill Hall, partly because it tries so hard to escape its 1970s ethos you can hear the seams creaking. But though the underlying dynamic is probably more lesbian feminist than anything else – or at least that's the impression it gives – the Drill Hall has a lot to offer the rest of us. It has a fully merited reputation as a venue for innovative lesbian and gay drama, having served as one of the focal points for radical theatre over the years. The difficult task it now has to perform is to retain that reputation while proving that politically aware drama doesn't have to consist of heavy-handed polemic. And there's some danger of stepping too far in the opposite direction. This is particularly the risk of arriving at saturation point in staging the 'paradox' that feminism can be funny too. That point was made in about 1978 by Victoria Wood, among others, and there is some hope that it may have sunk in by now.

But the Drill Hall does mount some tremendous productions – from successful experiments which have a gender-political edge to its role as the London house for Music Theatre London's camp, funny, and thoroughly worthwhile productions of Mozart, Puccini *et al*. Naturally, there can be a downside to adventurous programming, as anyone who sat through Opera Factory's long-overdue suicide production here in 1998 will testify. On balance, though, the successes justify the risks taken, and there is also a worthwhile and interesting education programme, with classes and workshops on a variety of physical and intellectual aspects of performance.

The auditorium is fairly small and very black – again much *à la* 1976 – but its breadth saves it from any sense of oppressiveness, and it is reasonably comfortable. For small-scale opera productions especially, the acoustic is good and the sightlines excellent.

Drill Hall

theatres and concerts

Drill Hall

The basement café tends towards the herbal-tea and vegan-sludge routine (though to be fair the pizza is genuinely delicious, if not particularly cheap). Also, at various times over the years it seems to have provided employment for some of the most disobliging and incompetent people in the world – as well, no doubt, as for some perfectly reasonable ones, but it's the others who stick in the mind. Oh, and it's unlicensed …

Upstairs in the bar, however (open on performance nights only), the perky staff provide good, quick service, while the place fills up with the usually quite camp and jolly, though very mixed, crowd of people who make up the Drill Hall's loyal following. AW

ADDRESS 16 Chenies Street, London WC1 (0171-631 1353)
OPEN bar 18.00–23.00 (Monday women-only); café 10.00–20.00
ACCESS tickets approximately £10–£12/£6 concessions
UNDERGROUND Tottenham Court Road, Warren Street

Drill Hall

theatres and concerts

Glyndebourne

You can't do Glyndebourne by halves. It's an over-the-top and quite expensive experience – so go the whole hog. The only man I've ever seen there who wasn't dressed as a waiter was actually a butler setting out silver candelabra on the picnic table of a rather grand party of 12. So, dig out the dinner jacket that you bought for some undergraduate function and haven't worn since. See if it fits, and if it doesn't, either lose some weight or buy a new one.

It is possible but fiddly to use public transport to go to Glyndebourne – for once I'd be inclined to throw principles to the wind and go by car. And get there early – the gardens really are lovely enough to warrant an extensive pre-opera stroll, the iced coffee is worth stopping for, and in any case you need to bag a picnic space for the interval.

Roughly speaking, the smaller formal gardens make for a slightly haughty picnic, while the main lawn is quite jolly, with the see-and-be-seen-by brigade (which unashamedly includes me) competing for the spaces along the ha-ha. The wild garden to the side is less busy, but has a super atmosphere of its own. Of course, if it rains the question of picnic spaces changes somewhat, as everybody fights for places on one of the outside terraces of the opera house itself. Don't worry about this, however, because even if it is raining when you arrive, the providence that looks after the English middle classes will ensure it has dried off by the time the interval comes.

Leaving aside the purely social aspects of Glyndebourne, there are other good reasons for going. The new auditorium has the best sightlines of any opera house in Europe or the US, and a fine, slightly dry acoustic. These characteristics combine with a sense of intimacy to generate an experience utterly unfamiliar if you're used to metropolitan grand opera houses. The reputation Glyndebourne has built among performers means

Glyndebourne

theatres and concerts

Glyndebourne

you are likely to hear singers here as starry as you will come across in any other performance space – though I don't think that autograph-hunting would be regarded as quite the thing, somehow. Also, I believe that the time allocated to rehearsals at Glyndebourne simply doesn't occur anywhere else these days. That's one more reason why you need to be prepared to extend the overdraft quite a lot in order to go. The performance you see at Glyndebourne will be, in purely technical terms, the best in the world. There is a curious corollary to this, which is that there may be some advantage in choosing relatively obscure works. In any case, tickets for Mozartian lollyhorses are incredibly difficult to get hold of, even though the legendary subscription-only days are now over. But because the investment all round in each production is so huge, there may be a tendency towards conservative production values where the more entrenched repertoire is concerned. Less well-known works carry less baggage with them, and so may be given more adventurous treatment.

OK, so it's all a huge, rather vulgar cliché, involving spending disgusting amounts of money on a single day's adventure. Stuff the petit-bourgeois moralising, admit that you're engaging in the politics of envy (otherwise known as sour grapes), and go for it big time. AW

ADDRESS Glyndebourne, Lewes, East Sussex (01273 813813)
OPEN May to August
ACCESS £10 to £124
BY ROAD from M25 follow M23 to Brighton, then A27 to Lewes (bypass), then A26 to Tunbridge Wells; fork right on to B2191 and follow signposts to Glyndebourne (map available from box office)
RAIL Lewes from London Victoria; some trains are met by coach (see Festival brochure)

Glyndebourne

theatres and concerts

Holland Park Music and Dance Festival

This is hardly Glyndebourne, but the opera and ballet festival that takes place each year from June to August in the ruins of Holland House has become a summer tradition. Be prepared to trust in the magic of theatre and music – even when you're convinced that the chorus of slaves from *Aïda* are wearing tea towels on their heads or when the park's tenor peacocks insist on joining in with Puccini's *La Bohème*. As you sit beneath your umbrella during the inevitable English summer downpour blowing your nose loudly in empathy for poor Mimi in her final throws, you will no doubt appreciate that such a setting renders opera truly democratic.

A post-festival stroll up and down the shady Holland Walk may lead to a romantic liaison, but only after some theatrical games of hide and seek among the benches and trees. WM

ADDRESS Holland Park, London W8 (0171–602 7856)
OPEN June to August
UNDERGROUND Holland Park/Kensington High Street

Holland Park Music and Dance Festival

theatres and concerts

Kenwood Music Festival

There is a certain ghastly wholesomeness about the Kenwood festival: people-carriers disgorging families probably referred to as 'tribes' by their mothers, in extreme cases carrying wicker picnic baskets. And do not get your musical expectations raised too high either. In the land of the jolly, the *1812* overture is king. Having said that, the setting is really lovely. From the Palladian front of Kenwood House, the grass sweeps down to a stretch of water, from the other side of which the orchestra plays. The trees, water and *trompe l'oeil* bridge form a wonderful backdrop for the music – much too good to be left to a heterosexual hegemony. Incidentally, if you can be bothered to get there early enough for Kenwood House still to be open, it's worth going in. It's largely an Adam number, with the kind of eighteenth-century elegant stone and plasterwork you would expect, but also take a look at the Orangery, and at the picture collection.

It used to be possible to avoid paying for these concerts simply by setting up camp on the 'wrong' side of the fence. But they've got wise to this and enlarged the enclosure, so I'm not sure that it's worth the effort any more – you might as well just grit your teeth and pay for the tickets.

You need to take a friend or two, a bottle of wine or two, and some tasty snacks. Get just a bit drunk and then abandon yourself to the sloppy romantic vulgarity of the whole experience. A suggested menu: champagne and smoked salmon or martinis and chilled soup – Rossini *The Thieving Magpie*; burgundy with pasta salad and cold roast something-or-other – Vivaldi *The Four Seasons*; Beaumes de Venise and tiramisu – Tchaikovsky *1812*.

Warm, pleasant, congenial ambience, shrubs, trees and flowers acquiring new scents and sharp outlines as the light changes from bright and unforgiving afternoon to louche evening – even the Emmas and Henrys begin to seem quite tolerable, the music sounds less like muzak,

Kenwood Music Festival

theatres and concerts

Kenwood Music Festival

and your friends start to look quite fanciable, though not half so much as the man over there with whom you've been exchanging sly glances for the past half hour. The music ends, and ... into the woods! AW

ADDRESS Kenwood House, Hampstead Lane,
London NW3
(0171-973 3427/413 1443)
OPEN July and August
UNDERGROUND Highgate

Kenwood Music Festival

Lyric Theatre

Neil Bartlett had an established reputation as a gay playwright, dramaturge and literary critic when he took over as artistic director of the Lyric, Hammersmith a few years ago. The Lyric itself was already an exciting theatre, having housed productions (including plays or adaptations by Bartlett himself) in which gender-fucking and explorations of sexuality went beyond the merely radical or chic. The appointment of Bartlett was an anti-marriage which has been blessed with high-achieving issue. Along with the Royal Court and the Drill Hall (see page 11.6), the Lyric has maintained sexuality as a theatrical issue which lives on challengingly beyond its absorption into mainstream theatre and television. (Remember that kiss in *EastEnders*?) But that doesn't mean the Lyric offers a purely polemical diet, banging on about muesli and oppression *à la* 1976. Instead, this is a theatre which remembers the theatrical and the outrageous, while still undertaking artistically serious and worthwhile productions, mainly of twentieth-century work, including some new writing.

Getting to the Lyric from Hammersmith Underground is a bit of a trial because it involves crossing Hammersmith Broadway, one of the most intimidating and anti-human victories of the motor car over civilisation. But persevere. Like practically every other decent theatre in London, the Lyric is for ever hanging by its fingernails over a chasm of bankruptcy, and it needs to keep the punters coming.

Inside, the main auditorium is a surprising survival of traditional red-plush-and-gilding late Victoriana, which was incorporated into the rebuild in the 1970s. The smaller Studio performance space was originally the most uncomfortably Spartan example of 1970s minimalism around, and to sit through a normal-length performance on those benches may have been good for the soul, but it was agony on the back

Lyric Theatre

theatres and concerts

Lyric Theatre

and the bum. Recent years have seen some concessions to the weakness of the flesh, however, and both the main theatre and the Studio are now comfortable enough.

The main bar and the restaurant occupy a big open space on the first floor of the building. It's a bit airportish in feel – the underfunding shows rather, here. But the food is not at all bad – simple but stylish sandwiches and salads. There is a down side, in that the openness of the space can encourage glares of vicious self-righteousness and histrionic 'coughing' fits from anti-smokers. But the staff are pleasant and helpful, the bar prices are not too high, and the other people frequently fun and sometimes attractive. The Lyric numbers more than its fair share of (resting?) actors among its audiences, and picturesque meetings between second and third spear carriers from old series of *Casualty* are fun to watch. So, overall, this is a good place: nice bar, and some of the most interesting theatre in London, much of it with a sexual political edge. AW

ADDRESS King Street, London W6 (0181-741 2311)
UNDERGROUND Hammersmith

Lyric Theatre

theatres and concerts

Music in Churches

Occasional recitals take place in churches all over London, and are worth looking out for, except for the ones that are dreadful. But the best regular events in the most interesting churches are probably the concert series in St John's Smith Square, St James's Piccadilly and St Martin-in-the-Fields, and the summer and winter music festivals in Christ Church Spitalfields.

The best route to St John's is by bus to the end of Whitehall, then on foot past the Houses of Parliament on one side and Westminster Abbey on the other, then to the start of Millbank and up Dean Stanley Street to Smith Square. St John's itself is a distinctive early-eighteenth-century building (known as Queen Anne's footstool, and if you take a quick look at the disposition of the four towers you'll see why) whose principal function now is as a concert hall. (Remember all those 'and now from St John's Smith Square' intros on the radio?) It presents programmes of serious music at its lunchtime and evening concerts, and has a good (if rather expensive) bar and restaurant in the basement.

If St Martin-in-the-Fields wasn't there, Trafalgar Square would be the dullest public space this side of Basildon. But the portico and steeple of St Martin's give a necessary grandeur and presence to the north-east corner of the square, and the interior of the church has a soothing churchiness and dignity. Many of the evening concerts have a 'baroque by candlelight' theme which can be pretty trying if taken to excess. But a concert on an early spring evening can be a lovely experience, with the outside darkening and the candles coming into their own, while a usually young and competent band plays Bach or Mozart. The downside is that the good works associated with the church include helping out a lot of homeless drunks without washing facilities and with an intimidating manner, so getting in to the church can be a bit of a trial.

Music in Churches

theatres and concerts

Music in Churches

Still ... the restaurant in the crypt is a bog-standard to goodish Church of England café, and at the end of the concert you have possibly (i.e. I don't know) the biggest concentration of gay pubs anywhere in Europe within easy walking distance.

The main thing about St James's Piccadilly is that it has a lovely interior – one of those simple, light Wren numbers which work so well, but on an unusually large scale. Also, the font is unusual and beautiful. The café to the south of the church is pretty indifferent, so you may do better to arrive early and have tea at Fortnum and Mason next door. There is also a rather nice but often desperately crowded pub around the corner off Jermyn Street to the south of the church. The most notable concerts are probably the early-music series, sponsored by a German airline – at least for those who like that sort of thing.

Hawksmoor's Christ Church Spitalfields is a completely wonderful building – the sheer stoneness of it survives to create a tense, ambiguous relationship with the ethereal aspirations of the steeple and the decoration (see page 5.6). With Scottish composer Judith Weir as artistic director, the summer and winter festivals offer music of a serious order indeed. Ticket prices range from the very reasonable to the really quite expensive, but the quality of the performances and the adventurousness of the programming make Christ Church an important musical venue in June and December. (And, in case that makes it all sound like slightly hard work, there is still a certain amount of camperie about – as when a few years ago during a rare performance of Britten's *Prodigal Son*, the entire front row could be observed to be craning its collective neck in an effort to look up the lead singer's cassock.) There used to be a bit of a sense of remoteness about Christ Church, but this has been significantly ameliorated by the double-edged sword of the gentrification of

Music in Churches

theatres and concerts

Music in Churches

the area, as a result of which there are some quite good cafés and bars in the former flower market up the road (see page 9.8), as well as other cultural goodies, including the local opera festival. AW

ST JOHN'S SMITH SQUARE
ADDRESS Smith Square, London SW1 (0171-222 1061)
UNDERGROUND Westminster

ST MARTIN-IN-THE-FIELDS
ADDRESS 5 St Martin's Place, London WC2 (0171-930 1538)
UNDERGROUND Trafalgar Square, Charing Cross

ST JAMES'S PICCADILLY
ADDRESS Piccadilly, London W1 (0171-734 4511)
UNDERGROUND Piccadilly Circus

CHRIST CHURCH SPITALFIELDS
ADDRESS Commercial Street, London E1 (0171-247 7202)
UNDERGROUND Liverpool Street, Old Street

Music in Churches

theatres and concerts

events

**Gay Pride/Summer Rites 12.2
Underwear Nights 12.6**

Gay Pride/Summer Rites

It's deepest dankest February as we go to press, so the festive delights of an English summer (fleeting at best) are a little difficult to imagine. But soon, come spring, the sap will stir and a young person's fancies will begin to look forward to what are supposed to be the twin highlights of the London gay calendar: Gay Pride and Summer Rites. Or maybe not.

London's Gay Pride has had mixed fortunes in recent years. Unlike cities with a strong carnival tradition, London has never quite resolved the relationship between the post-1960s out'n'proud street-demo side of things on the one hand and the ever-so-1980s party-in-the-park hedonism on the other. Things climaxed in 1997 with a march followed by the largest party ever on Clapham Common, the numbers swelled by hordes of straight couples with their children. The children, at least, could be forgiven for failing to recognise that this was supposed to be a celebration of alternative sexualities rather than a come-one come-all free festival.

And after the party, the inevitable come-down. Despite attracting nigh on 300,000 people, commercial sponsorship so high profile many felt demeaned by it, and beer prices that made the West End look cheap, it finally became clear that, yet again, Pride had made a substantial loss. Months of bickering and mutual recrimination followed.

1998 grasped the commercial dilemma by the horns and decided that the party in the park would, for the first time ever, be a ticket-only affair. Tickets went on sale in pubs and clubs all over the country; a relatively meagre 25,000 were sold. At the last minute the local council and the police decided that they, too, wanted a share of the bonanza and delivered substantial bills: suddenly, the maths looked silly. Pride 98 was cancelled.

Gay Pride/Summer Rites

events

Gay Pride/Summer Rites

But the march went ahead as planned, followed by a Reclaim-the-Streets-style occupation of the roads around Soho Square. The radicals declared it the best Pride ever, the party crowd felt hard done by.

Parallel to these events, the smaller and more intimate London-based Summer Rites festival was quietly thriving, seeming to many to offer everything Pride had lost.

Unlike Pride, where you expected to see everyone you'd ever fancied but only ever met that boring bloke you bumped into in Brighton, Summer Rites had a genuine community feel to it. (It began just three years ago as South London Pride.) For a post-political crowd, inured to spending upwards of a tenner to get into Trade, the modest entrance fee seemed cheap at the price. By deliberately restricting the scope of their ambition, and never pretending to offer anything other than a sunlit club on a summer's afternoon, Kim Lucas and Wayne Shires had cannily built a loyal following who eagerly looked forward to last year's Summer Rites in Brockwell Park as the perfect antidote to the fiasco that was Pride 98.

Unfortunately, it rained. And rained and rained and rained and rained: a wash-out.

Who can tell what will happen this year? As we go to press, a new-look 'Mardi Gras' Pride 99 in early July is being planned, with talk of closing off large parts of Soho for a street party coupled with a smaller party in a park at £10 a head. Summer Rites, we imagine, will book Brockwell Park in August once again and pray it doesn't rain.

If you want to visit London for one of these events, call Gay Switchboard (see page 0.10) to keep up to date with the latest plans. If you're already in the country, keep an eye on the gay press for further details. And, as ever, hope for the best and prepare for the worst. IM

Gay Pride/Summer Rites

events

Underwear Nights

Call me a pervert, but I really like Underwear Nights.

Even better, I like telling people about them, and watching them go slightly glassy-eyed as they try to compute the obvious advantages against the prospect of somebody you know seeing you, eek, in your scanties.

To the hardened pervert, of course, London's several and various Underwear Nights must seem desperately vanilla. No leather? No whips? No fist-fucking in slings with 18 people looking on? No thank you. But this is not really a fetish thang – if it were, I'd guess you'd see a rather more lavish selection of lingerie than the wall-to-wall Calvin Klein that predominates. Calvins plus, of course, the odd red satin jock-strap or downhome Marks and Sparks Y-fronts. Some people have no taste.

Not only are there a lot of people here you fancy, there's also a fair sprinkling of people who are, quite definitely, less attractive than you. And it doesn't matter. The body fascism that can be such a daunting aspect of the gay scene has much less force here. There's a much wider age range, and a noticeably wider choice of ethnic types than you'll see in most gay bars. And, when all's said and done, that plump bus conductor from Balham with the sagging crotch, just like you, had the balls to come into a club where he has to take his off clothes to get a drink at the bar. (Let's just hope you don't get his clothes back by mistake at the end of the night.)

The sex (did I mention the sex?) is similarly light-hearted. Maybe it's the faint air of public-school changing room that hangs about the place, or maybe it's an exhibitionist/voyeur *gestalt*, but you rarely see people shagging at an Underwear Night. (And I've looked.)

It's a gentlemen's excuse-me, and once you've filled your dance-card there's no greater pleasure than sitting in a darkened corner of the bar watching the people come and go, undressed like a Michelangelo. Good thesis material too: see how their left hand holds on to their beer on the

Underwear Nights

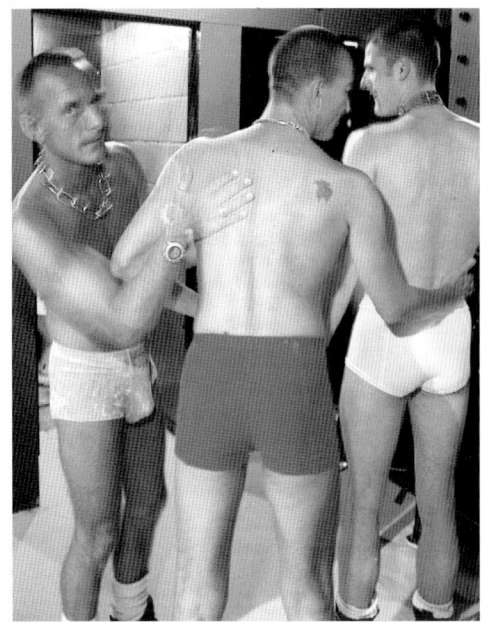

events

Underwear Nights

bar while their right toys absent-mindedly with their genitals. And the way those few people who already know each other stare fixedly at each other's faces, desperately avoiding a glance ... down there.

Pay your money on the door (it's rarely expensive) and you'll be given a black plastic bin-liner. Keep an eye out for a pile of small plastic money bags at this stage: there's nothing less attractive than standing at the bar on one foot shaking coins out of your boot.

Move confidently towards the dressing area and begin, calmly, to undress. If you had a spliff before you came (and it helps, it helps), think extra carefully about how you fold your clothes so your keys don't fall out of your pocket when you shove them in the bag.

Sort out just enough change to get you the number of drinks you expect to need, plus two. Crease your cigarette packet so it will fit into your sock without digging into your shin. Slip your cash bag into the top of one shoe, and your fags into the other. (Boots don't just look better than trainers, they hold more too.)

Hand your bag in at the coat check and take a moment to put your cloakroom ticket securely with your cash. Move to the bar and order your drink. Supping, leisurely turn to survey the crowd with a knowing yet attractively open expression. (Next week: 'Boots-only' Evenings.) IM

ADDRESS Y-Front at Substation South, 9 Brighton Terrace, London SW9
OPEN Mondays, 22.00–3.00 ACCESS free before 23.00/£3 after
UNDERGROUND Brixton

ADDRESS Underworld at The Block, 28 Hancock Road, London E3
OPEN Wednesdays, 22.00–3.00 ACCESS £3
UNDERGROUND Bromley-by-Bow

Underwear Nights

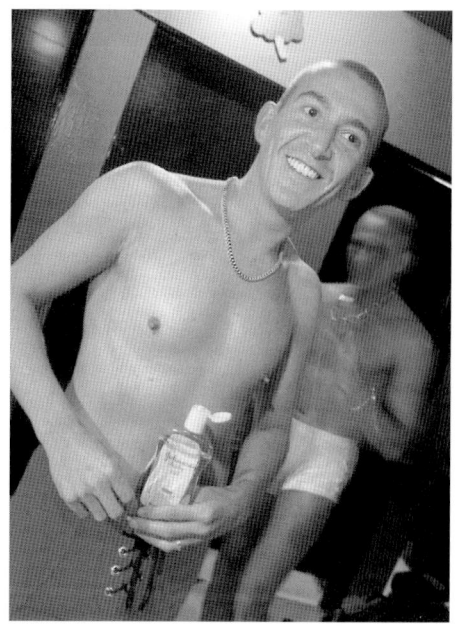

events

index

Index

Abney Park Cemetery 0.2, 6.2
Absolutely, *see* Substation South
Adonis Art 1.2
advertising revenue 0.0, 0.5
AIDS Treatment Project 0.6
Aitchison, George 10.6
All Hallows by the Tower 5.10
The Almeida 1.8
alternative scene 3.10
The Angel 1.8, 2.2
annual festivals 1.12
Aquarius Sauna 0.2, 7.2–7.4
Archway Sexual Health Clinic 0.6
The Artful Dodger 1.8
The Astoria 3.16
Auden, W H 10.18
Axiom News 0.4

Bachardy, Don 10.20
Backstreet 0.2, 3.2
Bacon, Francis 10.18
Bacon, Sir Francis 1.6
Balans 1.14
Balans West 0.1, 4.2–4.4
The Bar 2.12
Bar Code 2.30
Bartlett, Neil 11.20
Bass Taverns 2.30
Benjy's 2000 3.4
Berry Brothers and Rudd 8.14
Bhangra 3.8
bisexuality 1.16
The Black Cap 0.2, 2.4
The Block 3.6, 12.8
Bloomsbury Group 10.18

body fascism 12.6
Bogarde, Sir Dirk 10.20
Boswell, James 2.26
Boy George 7.16
Boystown 2.34
Boyz 0.4
Brick Lane 0.2, 9.2–9.4
British Library 10.2–10.4
Britten, Benjamin 1.6, 10.18, 11.26
Brixton
   No 7 Guesthouse 4.10
   Substation South 3.26
Brockwell Park 12.4
Brompton Cemetery 0.2, 6.4
Bromptons 1.4

cabaret 2.4, 2.6, 2.26, 2.28
Cafe Olé 1.10
Camden
   The Black Cap 2.4
   Camden Lock Market 9.6
   Camden Passage 1.8
   Zipper Store 9.6
Camden Lock Market 0.2, 9.6
Camden Passage 1.8
Canonbury Tower 1.6
Capital Gay 0.4
Cara Trust 0.6
Careline 0.10
Carrington, Dora 10.18
Central Middlesex Hospital 0.6
Central Station 0.1, 0.2, 1.8, 2.6
Centrepoint 2.22
Chapel Market 1.10
Charing Cross Hospital 0.6

Index

Chariots Roman Baths 7.6
Charminar Vegetarian 1.10
Chelsea Physic Garden 0.1, 5.2–5.4
chill-out 2.16, 2.28, 3.12
Christ Church Spitalfields 5.6, 11.26
City churches 5.6–5.16
Clapham Common 12.2
Clark, Michael 10.20
Clone Zone 1.2, 1.14
the closet 2.2, 4.10
Club Kali 3.8
Club V 3.10
Clune, Jackie 2.26
The Cock and Comfort 2.16
Coleherne 0.2, 2.8–2.10
Collins, Joan 10.20
Columbia Road Flower Market 0.1, 9.8–9.10
coming out 8.4
commercialism 0.2, 2.30, 3.16, 12.2
community 0.2, 1.2, 2.2, 2.6, 4.12, 12.4
The Complex 3.22
Comptons 1.14
Conway Hall 0.1, 11.2–11.4
Coward, Noël 10.18
Crafts Council of Great Britain 1.8
Croydon HIV Counselling and Testing Service 0.7
cruising 1.4, 1.14, 2.2, 2.10, 2.24, 3.6, 3.20

Davidoff's 8.12
Diana, Princess of Wales 4.6–4.8
Dirty Dishes, *see* Substation South
Divine David 2.26
do-it-yourself culture 3.10
The Dolphin 11.4
drag 2.4, 2.6, 2.16, 2.26, 2.32
drag queens 0.1, 1.12, 2.18, 2.24
dress codes 3.6
Drill Hall 0.1, 11.6–11.8
DTPM 3.12
Duckie 2.26
The Duke of Wellington 1.8

Ealing Hospital 0.7
Earl's Court 0.2, 1.2–1.4
  Adonis Art 1.2
  Balans West 4.2
  Bromptons 1.4
  Clone Zone 1.2
  Coleherne 2.8
  New York Hotel 4.8
  Philbeach Hotel 4.6
  Troubador Coffee House 4.4
East End
  Backstreet 3.2
  Benjy's 2000 3.4
  The Block 3.6
  Brick Lane 0.2
  Chariots Roman Baths 7.6
  The Cock and Comfort 2.16
  Columbia Road Flower Market 9.8–9.10
  The Joiners Arms 2.14
  The Royal Oak 2.14
  333 Old Street 2.14
  The White Swan 2.18
  York Hall 7.16
East End Pubs 2.12–2.18

gay london: a guide

Index

The Edward VI 1.8
The End 3.12
Erasmus, Desiderius 10.14
Estorick Collection of Modern Italian Art 1.8
exclusivity 1.12
Expectations 8.2

fetish 1.2, 1.14, 3.2, 8.2, 8.8, 8.10
First Out 0.0
FIST 3.2
Fitzgerald, Oswald 10.16
Floris 8.12
Forster, E M 10.18
Fortnum and Mason 8.14, 11.26
Freedom 1.16
The Fridge 3.18, 3.26
Fruit Machine, *see* Heaven

Gallipoli 1.10
GAY 3.14–3.16
the gay contribution 0.1
Gay's the Word 8.4–8.6
Gay and Lesbian Advice Directory 2.6
gay businesses 1.12, 4.2
gay entrepreneurs 0.2
'gay exhibition' 2.26
gay-friendly 1.6, 1.8, 4.2
gay lifestyle 1.12, 1.14, 3.22, 4.2
gay press, the 0.4–0.5, 1.2
Gay Pride 12.2–12.4
Gay Switchboard 12.4
'gay village' 0.2
gentrification 2.2, 11.26
ghetto 0.4

Gielgud, Sir John 10.20
GLAD 0.10
Glyndebourne 0.1, 11.10–11.12
Gough, Piers 10.18
Granita 1.8
Grant, Duncan 10.18
Greenwich District Hospital 0.7

Hall Carpenter Archives 0.10
Halliwell, Kenneth 1.6
Hampstead Heath 0.2, 2.24, 6.6, 7.8
Hawksmoor, Nicholas 5.6, 5.12, 11.26
Heaven 3.18–3.20, 3.26
history 0.0
HIV and AIDS support 2.6
Hockney, David 10.20
Holland Park Music and Dance Festival 0.1, 11.14
Howerd, Frankie 7.6

Ian Charleson Day Centre 0.8
ICARE 0.6
icons 1.12
infiltration 0.1, 4.4
Isherwood, Christopher 10.20
Islington 0.2, 1.6–1.10
  The Almeida 1.8
  The Angel 2.2
  The Artful Dodger 1.8
  Cafe Olé 1.10
  Camden Passage 1.8
  Canonbury Tower 1.6
  Central Station 1.8, 2.6
  Chapel Market 1.10
  Charminar Vegetarian 1.10

Index

Club v 3.10
Crafts Council of Great Britain 1.8
The Duke of Wellington 1.8
The Edward VI 1.8
Estorick Collection of Modern Italian Art 1.8
Gallipoli 1.10
Granita 1.8
Kavanagh's 1.8
The Kings Head 1.6
Lola's 1.8
Le Mercury 1.10
Le Montmartre 1.10
The Peasant 4.12
Popstarz 3.22
The Ram Club Bar 1.8
Regulation 8.10
Sadler's Wells 1.6
Union Chapel 1.8

Jack Straw's Castle 6.6
Jarman, Derek 10.20
The Joiners Arms 2.14
Jones' Dairy (Columbia Road) 9.10
Joseph, Jeremy 3.18

Kavanagh's 1.8
Kenwood House 11.16
Kenwood Music Festival 0.1, 11.16–11.18
Kew Gardens 5.18–5.20
Keynes, John Maynard 10.18
King's College Hospital 0.7
The Kings Head (Upper Street) 1.6
Kitchener of Khartoum, Earl 10.14–10.16

Kobler Clinic 0.7
Kruger, Suzie 3.2

Lawrence, T E ('Lawrence of Arabia') 10.16
leather 1.2, 1.14, 3.2, 8.2, 8.10
leather bars 2.8
the le cruisey effect 8.16
Leighton, Lord Frederic 10.6, 10.14
Leighton House 0.1, 10.6–10.8
Lloyds Building 5.8
Lobb 8.14
Lock's 8.14
Lola's 1.8
London Friend 0.10
Love Muscle 3.26
Lucas, Kim 12.4
Lyric Theatre 0.1, 11.20–11.22

macho 2.8
mainstream 1.12, 1.14, 2.2, 3.20, 3.22
Maugham, Syrie 8.12
The Men's Ponds, Hampstead Heath 7.8
Le Mercury 1.10
militaria 8.2, 8.10
Millennium Dome 5.24
mixed gay/straight 0.2, 1.16, 2.16, 3.20
mixed les/gay 0.2, 2.26, 3.10, 3.20, 7.10
Le Montmartre 1.10
Moore, Henry 5.12
Mortimer Market Centre 0.7
Museum of London 0.1, 10.10–10.12
Music in Churches 11.24–11.28
Music Theatre London 11.6
MX 0.4

gay london: a guide

Index

Nash, Thomas 6.2
National Portrait Gallery 0.1, 10.14–10.20
New Labour 1.6
New York Hotel 4.8
Nichols, Beverley 8.12
No 7 Guesthouse 4.10

Old Compton Café 1.14
Old Compton Street 0.2, 1.12–1.16
Opera Factory 11.6
Orton, Joe 1.6
Outlook Lesbian and Gay Talking Directory 0.11
Owen, Wilfred 10.16

PACE 0.11
Paxton and Whitfield 8.12
Pears, Peter 1.6, 10.18
The Peasant 0.1, 4.12
Philbeach Hotel 4.6–4.8
Pink Paper, The 0.4, 8.6
pink pound 0.2, 1.8, 2.30
Pizza Express 1.10
Poems, Chloe 2.26
Popcorn, *see* Heaven
poppers 1.4
Popstarz 3.22–3.24
porn 1.2, 1.14, 3.6, 8.2
post-gay 0.4
post-political 12.4
The Princess Louise 11.4
Princess of Wales conservatory (Kew Gardens) 5.20
Prowler Store 8.8

public spaces 1.14, 3.20

Q Cars 3.28
Queen Mary's University Hospital 0.7
queer anarchists 1.12, 3.10
Queer Nation, *see* Substation South
QX 0.4

radical theatre 11.6, 11.20
The Ram Club Bar 1.8
Reader's Wifes 2.26
red-light district 1.12
Regulation 8.10
Ricketts, Charles 10.14
Rogers, Richard (Lord Rogers of Riverside) 5.8
The Royal Free Hospital 0.8
The Royal London Hospital 0.8
The Royal Oak 2.14, 9.10
The Royal Vauxhall Tavern 0.1
rubberwear 1.2, 1.14, 8.2, 8.10

Sadler's Wells 1.6
safer sex 6.6, 7.2
Sailors Sauna 2.18
St Bartholomew's Hospital 0.8
St Botolph's, Aldgate 5.6
St Dunstan's 5.12
St George's Hospital 0.8
St James's 8.12–8.14
St James's Piccadilly 11.26
St John's Smith Square 11.24
St Katherine Cree 5.8
St Magnus the Martyr 5.12
St Margaret Pattens Eastcheap 5.10

Index

St Martin-in-the-Fields 11.24
St Mary's Hospital 0.8
St Mary Aldermary 5.14
St Mary at Hill 5.12
St Mary le Bow 5.14
St Mary Woolnoth 5.12
St Paul's Cathedral 5.14
St Stephen Walbrook 5.12
St Vedast-alias-Foster 5.14
Sassoon, Siegfried 10.18
the scene 0.0, 2.22, 3.20, 3.30
scoring 1.4
second-hand books 8.6
Selfridges 8.16–8.18
sex shops 1.12, 8.2, 8.8
Sexual Offences Act 10.20
Shannon, Charles 10.14
Shires, Wayne 3.26, 12.4
Sir John Soane's Museum 0.1, 10.22–10.24
sleaze 2.8
SM dykes 2.6
Smith, Chris 1.6, 10.20
Soane, Sir John 10.22
Soho 0.2, 2.32
   Balans 1.14
   Clone Zone 1.14
   Comptons 1.14
   Freedom 1.16
   Old Compton Café 1.14
   Old Compton Street 1.12–1.16
   Prowler Store 8.8
   The Village Soho 1.16
The Soho Athletic Club 7.10
Soundshaft 3.26

The Spiral 2.12, 2.16
Stoney Parson's stained-glass workshop 9.10
Strachey, Lytton 10.18
strippers 2.6, 2.18, 2.26
Substation South 3.26–3.28, 12.8
Summer Rites 12.2–12.4
Swift, Jonathan 2.26

Tatchell, Peter 5.8
The Terrence Higgins Trust 0.6
Thames Barrier 5.24
Thames Boat Trip 5.22–5.24
theme nights 3.26
333 Old Street 2.14
Toolbox, *see* Substation South
Trade 3.30, 12.4
tradition 2.12, 2.16, 2.26
Troubador Coffee House 4.4
Truman's Brewery 9.2
Turnmills, *see* Trade
TV/TS night 4.8

unassimilated queer culture 2.30
underwear nights 12.6–12.8
Underworld, *see* The Block
Union Chapel 1.8
University College Hospitals Group 0.9
Up Pompeii 7.6

Vale Press 10.14
The Village Soho 1.16
visibility 0.2, 2.22, 2.30, 7.12

Warhol, Andy 10.20

gay london: a guide

Index

Weir, Judith 11.26
Whipps Cross Hospital 0.9
The White Swan 2.18
Wilde, Oscar 10.6, 10.14
Wilde About Oscar, *see* Philbeach Hotel
Wildlife, *see* Heaven
Wilson, Colin St John 10.4
Wodehouse, P G 8.12
Wolfenden, Jeremy 10.20
Wolfenden, John 10.20
Wolfenden Report on Homosexual Offences and Prostitution 10.20
women-only 2.2, 2.26
Wood, Victoria 11.6
Wren, Sir Christopher 0.1, 5.6, 5.10, 5.12

Y-Front, *see* Substation South
YMCA 7.12–7.14
York Hall 7.16

Zipper Store 9.6

PICTURES
Photographs by Heike Löwenstein except:
Keith Collie: pages 10.3 and 10.5
National Portrait Gallery, Andrew Putler: pages 10.15, 10.17, 10.19, 10.21
Mike Hoban: pages 11.11–11.13
Lyric Theatre, Mike Laue: pages 11.21–11.23

Beautiful Twisted Night

'Prostitutes, hustlers, porn stars, strippers, gangsters, pimps, dominatrixes, trans-sexuals, madams, subculture celebrities, superstars and even Satan worshippers' dance in and out of Marc Almond's 'beautiful twisted night'. Here, in a collection of his poetry, prose and lyrics of the last 20 years, is the city as a 'playground of fantasy and desire.'

Beautiful Twisted Night is a hard and loving look at the city streets, the red-light districts, the clubs and bars, the gay cultures and subcultures. It chronicles the dreams and disappointments of the city's inhabitants from the recognisable – Saint Judy – to the anonymous 'flotsam, jetsam, bottom-of-the-bin angels' – Exotica Rose, Jamie Dream, Champagne – from the bordello to the high-rise. 'With selected lyrics from every album he's ever recorded (plus a few he hasn't), fans certainly won't be disappointed.' Paul Burston, *Time Out*

ISBN 1 84166 023 X
PRICE £12.00 (paperback)

Marc Almond

also available from ellipsis